2/3/06

To School #84 -
Thanks!
Wishes -

Harmony,

Hallie Bryan

Hallie's Comet

Breaking the
CODE

HALLIE'S COMET

Breaking the
CODE

What Successful People Know and What
Others are Trying to Find Out

A Strategic Approach to Managing Your Personal
Life for Business and Personal Success

Hallie Bryant, former Harlem Globetrotter

and

O'Merrial Butchee, CEO of Visionamics, Inc.

Book I of III
The Harmony Series
DTE PRODUCTIONS

84

Visionamics, Inc.
DTE PRODUCTIONS
The Harmony Series
P.O. Box 3264
Munster, IN 46321
(219) 938-3114

Drawings and Cover Designed by Dr. Gregory Bell
Photographs by: Craig Arive of the Indianapolis Monthly,
Rich Voorhees, Master of Photographic Imaging of
Logansport, Indiana, and Robert Welborn of Montclair,
New Jersey

DTE Productions is a registered trademark of Visionamics, Inc.

Printed in the United States of America by
R.R. Donnelley & Sons Company

Library of Congress Cataloging-in-Publication Data
is available.

ISBN 0-9724894-0-1

CONTENTS

Contents

QUOTATION SECTION:
POST BOOK INTERVIEWS

"We all should read this book to investigate our inner feelings and thought processes. This would let us feel good about communicating with others and help to determine the importance of why we are here.

I am very pleased that I know Hallie Bryant for he has been a guiding light for Oscar Robertson. Hallie, at guard, became a hero for me to emulate and match his accomplishments. I would sit and watch his movements, footwork, mannerisms, and grace. I wanted to be that player, Hallie Bryant."

Oscar "Big O" Robertson
Elected to the NBA Hall of Fame
Twelve-time NBA All-Star (1961–72)

"In the more than 30 years I have known Hallie Bryant, I have been impressed by the knowledge he has gained and how it applies to daily life. As a Harlem Globetrotter, he has observed life from an interesting viewpoint. In this book the reader can gain helpful suggestions and enjoy Hallie's *Hallieisms*."

Jerry Colangelo
Chairman and CEO
The NBA Phoenix Suns
The Arizona Diamondbacks Baseball Team
2001 Major League Baseball World Series Champions

"Hallie Bryant's story is an excellent testimony to the benefits of hard work, principled living and a good heart. In the rich tradition of Indiana schoolboy hoop stars, Hallie filled the shoes inspirationally as a global ambassador for his family, his state and his country. The 'Trotters' history would not be the same were it not for the contribu- tions of Hallie Bryant."

Julius "Dr. J" Erving
Vice President, Orlando Magic
Elected to the Basketball Hall of Fame

"If you want to develop concepts that can assist you in life you will love, Hallie's Comet—Breaking the CODE. Interesting is Hallie's de- scription of courage. Read it—you will come away energized."

Dick Vitale
Sports Commentator for ESPN and ABC Sports
ESPN's First-ever NCAA Basketball Announcer

"I know from a personal view that the principles in this book work. There were times when Hallie and I were roommates, as Harlem Globetrotters, I would search our hotel room for him. I would find that he had isolated himself to study.

I asked Hallie to help me to recognize things that would provide harmony in my life. He gave me some invaluable guidance and I have grown. You, too, will profit greatly by reading and studying the blue- print set forth in this book."

Meadowlark Lemon
Former Harlem Globetrotters'
"Clown Prince of Basketball"

"Breaking the CODE gives you a series of practical, purposeful steps you can take immediately to improve every aspect of your life."

Brian Tracy
Author, "Victory!"

"So many motivational writers use sports analogies to illustrate good and bad business behavior, and too often the analogies ring false be- cause the analogies are often cliché and impersonal.

Hallie Bryant knows the world of sports and business intimately, so when he talks about the importance of teamwork, the power of passion or the feel for vision, his words carry special meaning. He knows how the lessons of sports apply to the world of business, because he has had success in both worlds. The things he has learned can instruct us all."

Jeff Smulyan
Chairman and CEO
Emmis Communications

"Part reminiscence, part play book, Break the CODE is a slam-dunk of ideas and inspiration from someone who represents the American Dream in the classiest and finest way. Do yourself a favor and enjoy the easy style and practical suggestions that lie within. It will help you create a better life."

Lou Heckler
Motivational Speaker

"In *Hallie's Comet-Breaking the CODE,* Hallie Bryant describes in easy to understand concepts the knowledge and skill sets one must develop to achieve success in life or business.

Perhaps the most important message in the book deals with the 'positive attitude' a person must develop and maintain to achieve personal goals. Filled with 'Hallieisms' the book will show you how to break the CODE."

Rene R. Champagne
Chairman of the Board
And Chief Executive Officer ITT

"[I] Suggest all CEOs and all corporate employees make it a must to read—Great reading by Hallie 'The Comet' Bryant."

Red Klotz
Owner—Head Coach
Red Klotz Sports Enterprises

"Hallie and O'Merrial are two of the smartest people I know. Their unique insights to assist all of us, I know, come from great depth of study, and understanding . . . and a sincere desire to communicate that depth . . . to lift you and me."

Arnold "Nick" Carter
Vice President, Communications Research
Nightingale-Conant Corporation

"To give a resounding endorsement of this book requires no effort on my part. One has only to enter a dialog with this consummate teacher or listen to him as he communicates with other people to realize that he is a master presenter.

His perspicacity, sincerity and obsession to be understood surge to the surface when he expounds his concepts and precepts. These traits are manifest in this book which should be a reading requirement for all aspirants to greater things."

Gregory Bell, DDS
Director, Dental Services, Logansport State Hospital
1956 Olympic Gold Medallist—Long Jump

"This is a book that should be read many times—study it. It's worth it. You will live easier and better."

"It is inspirational. It was an 'easy read.' There were short segments with phrases, word plays, boxed images and some personal examples. I especially liked the stories about your father and your dog. Your personal sympathy, empathy and feeling of 'tikun olum,' (Jewish for *repair the world*) shine through beautifully. Keep up the good work."

Dr. Charles and Barbara Coffey
Founder of Harmony Basketball Tournament
In Pittsburgh, Pennsylvania

"Hallie doesn't break the code—he writes the code for success in life."

Lyn St. James
7-time Indy 500 Driver
Author, "Ride of Your Life"

"Hallie's book is an excellent and easily accessible workbook of techniques for positive self-development related to all age groups. We have conducted workshops together combining his concepts with mine regarding the jazz components of melody, harmony, rhythm and improvisation. The enthusiastic reactions and responses by the students are absolutely exhilarating."

Larry Ridley
Jazz Artist, Professor of Music, Emeritus, Rutgers University

"If you've ever wondered about the 'what, why, and how' of personal success, the answers are here. Hallie's empathetic style and fresh perspectives make getting better, fun again. Makes you want to go for it— and shows you how!"

Dr. Shad Helmstetter
Author, "What To Say When You Talk To Yourself"

ACKNOWLEDGMENTS

From Hallie Bryant:

First of all, I am most grateful to the almighty Creator, God, because with God all things are possible. I am writing this book because of the persistent urgings of many people, especially at the conclusions of my speaking and performing presentations. Writing this book has allowed me to understand why a thankful heart has a continuous feast. I am truly thankful to all of the wonderful and thoughtful people who contributed to this book and supported me in this endeavor. I would fill a book if I listed all the names of people who have touched my life. Since that is not practical, I send a universal heartfelt "thank you" to all of you. *You know who you are and I love and appreciate you.*

There are a few people that I acknowledge who have been guiding forces, advisors, and instruments in my growth, development, and completion of this book.

Attorney Clarence Doninger has been my legal counsel and loyal friend for many years. I thank Bill Shover, the writer of the foreword and editor of this book, for his brilliant editing skills, guidance, and support. I thank him not only for his support in working with me in editing this book, but for his support since my senior high school days. Whenever I have needed him he has always come through for me. Dr. David Cain is my personal friend and number-one medical advisor. Dr. Chuck Coffey philosophizes with me about these concepts on a regular basis. Dr. Freeman Martin is a kindred spirit and true family friend. Dr. Greg Bell has given to me unconditional friendship. His input in all areas of this book is invaluable. Arnold "Nick" Carter is my good friend, communication coach, and talking "buddy" from Nightingale-Conant Corporation, Chicago, IL. Les and Edna May Johnston compiled my life's story in *The Scrap Book*. This book was a vital resource for my book. Meadowlark Lemon who was my Harlem Globetrotter teammate and remains my close friend who reminisced with me to bring forgotten events back to life. Tom Binford, who was the track Chief Steward for the 500-mile Indianapolis Motor Speedway, was the consummate business man and mentor. He taught me business sense and the power of living with purpose.

Other associates who contributed to this book with their support and encouragement are:

Art Angotti   Mack McKenzie
Joseph Anzivino   William "Bill" Mason
"Sweet" Charlie Brown   Robert Montgomery
David Allen Bryant   Don Odle
Donna Johnston-Burchick   Clifford Robinson
Coach Ray Crowe   Judy Rogers
Art Dixon   Judy Shepherd
Bruce Flanagan   Al Spurlock
Debie Friedman   Bill Warner
"Wee" Willie Gardner   Ed Whitehead
Cleveland Harp   Jack Whiteman
Richard "Dick" Lacy   Larry "Homer" Williams
Norman "Jr." Lee   Raymon and Jeanne Wilson
Bernard McFadden   Rev. Ty Wilson

I would like to convey my very best wishes to Mannie Jackson, Owner and Chairman of the Harlem Globetrotters and to the entire staff. May the team continue their unrivaled legacy of good will ambassadors to the world.

Govoner Vaughn, thanks for the constant updates of Globetrotter activities.

And, finally, I thank my immediate family who is responsible for my rock-solid foundation: L. Deloris Hayes is a truly beautiful, gifted and talented woman. As my partner in life, Deloris has allowed me to be fully who I am—a free spirit. I thank God for her. I thank my extended family including Attorney Sherri R. Sawyer and Kathy L. Hayes for making my personal life complete; my parents Calvin and Julia Mae Bryant (both deceased); stepmother Katie Bryant; brothers William J. Bryant deceased, Thomas J. Bryant who has been like a surrogate father, as well as, a loving brother; my sisters, Lillian A. Boyd and Evelyn Carter; Cousin Lizzie Raindrop who was my surrogate mother from the time of my mother's death when I was five years old, and her family; my mother's five sisters of which only one is still with us: Aunt Sallie L. Davis; Cousin Mamie Isom, still well at the age of 101 years young; and Cousin Louella Walker's family.

No one person can "do it" alone. Even when you think you can, you are never alone, and you cannot stop the external influences from impacting your life and your decisions. Outside forces are helping you with or without your permission.

This book possibly would not have been written without O'Merrial Butchee. Her rare integrity, honesty, trust and intellect allowed me to be spontaneous and free-flowing with my ideas and concepts for this non-fictional book. I thank her as the co-author of this book.

From O'Merrial Butchee

When people say that they have done it all on their own, it is my opinion that they just do not understand the Big Picture called *life*. These people identify with the term *bootstrappers* who are people who think that they accomplish tasks and achieve goals on their own efforts, skills and abilities. I would be committing an egregious error if I did not remind the bootstrappers that there are invisible and/or unseen forces constantly assisting them along their journey. The unawareness of these forces does not mean that they do not exist.

Sometimes we can feel extremely lonely and alone as we take on life's challenges in our struggle for success, but we must realize that we are never alone. There are powers greater than ourselves constantly working, praying, and assisting us on our journey. I am thankful for the invisible and/or unseen forces in my life.

First, I thank God for giving me wisdom and knowledge and the privilege of sharing it with you. I have too many friends and supporters to acknowledge, therefore I will give a heartfelt "thank you" to all of you. However, I must give special acknowledgement to a few individuals that helped me with the completion of this book. They are Charlie Mitchell who continues to keep me balanced; William, Marvin, and Martin Butchee who are my brothers and consistent in supporting me;

and my father (deceased) who inspired me to go after my dreams.

A special thanks go to my mother, Richie Mae, who made her transition before the completion of this book. Thank you *Moma* for your support and always believing in me.

FOREWORD

Bill Shover

When I first met Hallie Bryant, our "Mr. Basketball," he was a thoughtful, calm, and introspective man, much more mature than his 18 years.

During the time I was the game director of the Indiana All-Star Basketball Team, I informed Hallie that he had been elected the "Number 1" player in basketball-crazy Indiana. Each summer since 1940, Indiana's finest high school players played Kentucky's finest in a charity classic for the visually impaired.

Hallie, then and now, was reserved, shy, humble and deeply serious. While he was a freshman varsity basketball player at Indiana University on scholarship, I needed to borrow Hallie's All-Star jacket. I went to his home on Hiawatha Street in Indianapolis. The street, home, and neighborhood no longer exist—casualties of urban renewal.

By today's standards, Hallie's home was a hovel. I will always remember the look in his eyes. Ashamed of the poverty condition but resolute and determined to take himself to a better life. Hallie has never referred to the poverty of his childhood, only saying that "his family was rich in love."

After three seasons of playing in the Big 10 and graduation, a professional career in the National Basketball Association loomed. In 1957 the NBA offered few opportunities for Blacks. Instead, Hallie joined the Army and served two years as a lieutenant. He received an honorable discharge and became a member of the Harlem Globetrotters. In his 27 years as a "Trotter," Hallie traveled world-wide and learned that people were much alike and could melt inhibitions through playing in Hallie's "Harmony Circle," which is the physical interactive presentation to Hallie's Wheel of Harmony.

His career with the Globetrotters as a player and team executive, is among the longest tenure. As a motivational speaker, and "edutainer" (teacher and enter-

tainer), Hallie inspires people to develop their full potential.

In this book, a simulated one-on-one with Hallie,
the reader can relate experiences. His philosophical ob-
servations are a mosaic of life itself. This look into my
friend Hallie may open passages in your life, provide
inspiration and happiness.

BILL SHOVER
Retired Executive
The Indianapolis Star
The Arizona Republic and
The Phoenix Gazette

What the eyes see and the ears hear,
if seen and heard often enough,
will be remembered
and becomes part of us - A HABIT

Hallie "The Comet" Bryant

Topics

Life is a process—an unfolding. All of life is like a river flowing. Do not hinder the flow. As you grow and develop you will become a rich resource of information. You will be the sum total of all your teachers, mentors, coaches, writers, authors, and philosophers that you have had the privilege of meeting or studying. Like you, we, too, are a reflection of those individuals we have studied. Some of the great authors and philosophers who have become a part of our experience are as follows: James Allen, Robert Anthony, Dr. Ken Blanchard, Dr. Venice Bloodworth, Dr. Richard Carlson, Richard Carson, Arnold "Nick" Carter, Dr. DeePak Chopra, Rev. Johnnie Coleman, Stephen Covey, Bert Decker, Dr. Wayne Dyer, Guy Finley, Shadrick Helmstetter, Napoleon Hill, Vernon Howard, Dr. William James, Dr. Spencer Johnson, Ken Keyes, Ernie Larsen, Dr. Maxwell Maltz, Og Mandino, Earl Nightingale, Dr. Ulwyn Pierre, Jim Rohn, Don Miguel Ruiz, Mark Sanders, Dr. Bernie Segal, Dr. B.F. Skinner, Brian Tracy, and of course, *The Bible.*

There is nothing new under the sun. Therefore, we are not presenting this material as if we just discovered the fountain of youth. However, we have tapped into a "WOW"—a Well of Wisdom. In this writing, you will read quotes from other authors, adaptations of training modules or models, and language from other sources infused with our researched perspectives. We leap-frog over the hype and offer the wisdom that can move you towards successes by breaking the **CODE**.

Breaking the CODE is our effort to 1) assist you in self-management concepts for focused thinking, acting purposefully, and controlling your energy; 2) creating the kind of life that you desire for yourself, and 3) self-reliance concepts that will enable you to take control and responsibility of your outcomes. The CODE is the information that successful people know. Hallie breaks the CODE by revealing to you what others need to know about the CODE for personal and professional successes. How well you mesh together the "CODE" (Coordination, Organization, Direction, and Energy) with your thoughts, words, and actions or what we refer to as your habits, will determine your level of success. This is what many successful people who are living a pleasing life know and what others are trying to find out. By the way, we will not define success for you and no one else can. You must determine what success means to you.

The topics are presented in a simple ready-to-use conversational format and will give you *practical solutions* and *tools* to assist you in taking responsibility for your success. Success is a mindset. Success is a process. To get beyond where you presently are, it may be time for examining your usual way of thinking and doing things. If you are looking for different results then perhaps, it is time to make a paradigm shift because doing the same thing repeatedly expecting different results is called insanity. A paradigm shift is a fundamental change or shift in your normal thinking pattern, approach, or philosophy. It may be one change or any combination of the three. Once you can see things from many perspectives, you become a master re-framer. The mind begins to be open to new possibilities and eliminate CODE blockers. **YES!**™

HOW TO USE THIS BOOK

"Take a Sip from the WOW!"

HALLIE BRYANT

The Well of Wisdom—"WOW"

This book will be that resource, or well, that you will go to for a sip, an occasional drink, or a bucket. It will depend on your thirst for knowledge or your needs at that time. We will break some of the unwritten rules of the game called *Life*. Many of the unwritten rules evolved out of necessity. Some of those rules no longer apply to your present situation, however you find yourself still abiding by them. Your past is not your potential. It is time to toss some of those CODE blockers (outdated rules, unwarranted fears, old beliefs, etc.) into the river like unwanted fish. YES!™

We will be using the word you a great deal in this book because this book is about you. It is a personal journey of introspection. At first, read for clarity and information. Later will come the understanding. Allow yourself to slip into the GAP. The GAP that represents the place in between the thoughts known as the silence. The GAP is the place where there is quiet, which allows serenity, peace, and creativity to co-exist.

Initially, place acceptance of the principles on the backburner. What we ask is for you to allow yourself to hear and be receptive to different ways of hearing and seeing things. Like any major, effective change, breaking the CODE is a process. As you read through this material we ask that you remember to RBMG—Relax, Breathe, and Move Gracefully and you will come to know! Of course, RBMG which induces inner harmony is a Hallieism that you will often see in this book. This is worth keeping and one that will get you through your most stressful moments. Relax, Breathe, and Move Gracefully. You will also see YES!™ sprinkled throughout the book. YES!™ is another Hallieism. It is an acronym meaning Your Energy Source™. We will discuss YES!™ as a powerful motivational tool in Section VII.

In short, in the words of the late Bob Collins, sports editor for The Indianapolis Star, "hear us now, believe us later." In not only viewing this book, but in all you read, 1) simply read it, 2) read and relate it to something you know, then 3) read it and expand the ideas or concepts to what you know. A moment's insight can be worth a whole lifetime of experience.

Why is it important to grasp it now? "Don't forget that Hallie, the Comet, doesn't come around too often." Bob Collins wrote that quote often in his newspaper columns when he was covering a game. In fact, he gave me the nickname "The Comet" after Halley's Comet. Photograph A, on the next page, is a picture of me standing on the court reliving my introduction as an athlete.

I can hear the voices of Tom Carnegie and Sid Collins announcing, "6 feet 3 inches tall from Indiana University, Mr. Basketball, Hallie 'The Comet' Bryant."

Photograph A

BOOK FORMAT

This book is inspiring, educational, informative, and entertaining. We firmly believe that you create success from within and that what constitutes success is personally defined. This book puts you in action immediately. You are under construction and growing. There is no need to give yourself a hard time—so talk tenderly to yourself. *Hallie's Comet—Breaking the CODE* is a book presented in conversational tone. It is not a finger pointing or blaming document. It is a combination of many years of open-minded research, experiences in the trenches, and in-depth study and observation of successful and unsuccessful people. Yes, we said unsuccessful people. Unsuccessful people are successful people in the making. To act as if these people do not exist is playing the hype game. We believe in acknowledging what is true and moving onward. It is the truth that sets us free.

Hallie's Comet—Breaking the CODE is the first of a three-part series aimed at self-actualization or personal growth and development. This book is a worker's tool-box that will provide the materials needed to get you through the process. Remember, as author Vernon Howard says, "If it's your work it will be your reward." The second book will be about professional growth and development. Book three will discuss personal relationships. We acknowledge that it is almost impossible to separate the personal from professional growth and development. It is also difficult to discuss relationships without discussing personal growth and development issues; therefore, there will be some overlapping and intermingling of concepts and principles in all three books. Each book may be used either separately or as reinforcement for the other. The aim and focus of each book will be governed by the key topic discussed which enhances self-mastery and self-reliance.

Hallie's Comet—Breaking the CODE has been deliberately chosen to lead this series because the only thing you can fix is yourself. Your life will become more manageable once you identify those unwritten rules and behaviors that are keeping you from moving forward.

This journey will give you insights into the "rules of the game" called Life and will give you the tools you will need to help you to implement them. *Hallie's Comet—Breaking the CODE* is a precious gem that will mean something different to everyone who studies it.

Breaking the CODE is woven together by refined stories and events that add clarity to universal truths. This information is presented in many tones. It is divided into eight sections of which the first four sections discuss the basics of the CODE—Coordination, Organization, Direction, and Energy. The *Half-time Show* is provided in an entertaining sneak preview format of some of Hallie's scrapbook moments. Section V summarizes Hallie's Habits, Section VI gives you tools for learning, and Section VII is devoted to giving you affirmations and tools to make many of the Hallieisms and principles "stick." Section VIII brings it all together and empowers you to move forward with the Post-Game Interview. In addition, some chapters will have their key points summarized on an "anchor tool" called a "TIMEOUT."

Understand that we enjoy life and have fun with life. So you will see a humorous approach to some of these concepts; however, the humor is no indication that what we say is to be taken lightly. As I recall my days as a Harlem Globetrotter, no one brought more humor to the group than my dear friend Meadowlark Lemon as seen with me in Photograph B. Also during the same era, many fans did not realize that there were more than one Globetrotter unit on the circuit. Two other super-talented Globetrotters that delighted the audiences, were my friends Bob "Showboat" Hall as seen with me in Photograph C and Hubert "Geese" Ausbie who is seen with me and Marques Haynes in Photograph D. Even though much of what we did on the court looked like mere fun to the viewer, it was intense work combined with talent and endurance.

So with that, enjoy the journey—

Let Go, Lighten Up, and Let God.

Meadowlark Lemon and Hallie Bryant

Photograph B

BOB "SHOWBOAT" HALL   HALLIE BRYANT

Bob "Showboat" Hall and Hallie Bryant

Photograph C

Hubert "Geese" Ausbie, Hallie Bryant, and Marques Haynes

Photograph D

PRE-GAME TALK

"Hallie, take out from the river what you need.
Everything taken from this river isn't meant to be eaten."

CALVIN BRYANT

As I sit here with my collaborator and friend, O'Merrial Butchee, the tune and the words to the song, *Summer-time,* are echoing in my ears—"the fish are jumpin' and the cotton is high." It takes me back to the days when I was just a little boy in the rural South. We lived in a small village called Calhoun Falls, South Carolina about 12 miles from Abbeville, South Carolina (or as we used to say about a wagon distance away). Abbeville is located about fifty three miles from Augusta, Georgia. I marveled over having many special places to hide and think. Now, with the hustle and bustle of the city or being stuck on a crowded bus or airplane, there are few places for solitude. In those days, I would go to the woods, cornfields, or fishing holes to collect my thoughts. I fondly remember going to the bank of one of the tributaries or branches that ran from the Savannah River to meditate—a place where I felt like a king.

My father, Calvin, used to take me fishing during the day. I thought I was special because I had my father all to myself. I did not realize that every one else was in school or working at that particular time. I think we all want to feel special and be special to someone.

Loving family members always surrounded me. I was the middle child and I had two older brothers and two younger sisters. My mother passed away when I was five years old. That is probably why I felt so special, because I saw my father being both mother and provider to us all, for a period of time, and he still had time to take me fishing. My aunts became surrogate mothers until my father married a very special woman named Katie. Together my entire family formed a support system, which reminds me that it truly "takes a village to raise a child."

I had many happy moments as a child, but one that stays with me is when I caught my first fish. My father and I were sitting on the bank with our fishing poles in the water. The cane poles were made from bamboo and they had a line of cord string, a cork as a floater, and a lead-sinking hook extending from them. I snagged that fish and it made me feel good knowing that my father was there to witness it. That day I made my daddy proud, at least, I thought so. It did not matter that it took two or three more times to actually land a fish. I was so excited about the first fish I snagged, I pulled it from the water with so much force that I flung it somewhere up in the trees behind us.

We would sit at the fishing hole with our feet dangling in the water as the refreshing southerly breeze blew over our bodies bringing all that mother nature had to offer, including the sand, dirt and bugs. We would swat at the flies and mosquitoes and between the swats we would talk and just experience life.

Now I understand the wisdom of "Papa," which I affectionately called my father. Papa taught me how to fish, hunt, and to plant seeds in Mother Earth and harvest what I had sown. He also taught me to love all people because we are all God's children. These lessons have served me well.

My father had very little formal education but he was as wise as the wise old owl. Now that I think about it, he was my first WOW (Well of Wisdom). He was a religious man who believed in doing right. He taught me about integrity, responsibility, pride, and love for self and others. He could have handed me the fish he caught but he spent our quality time teaching me to fish. He said, "Hallie, take out from the river what you need. There are some things that you will pull out that you won't need. Don't be greedy, throw them back. Be considerate of the next man to cast his pole. Become aware of unhealthy things. Everything taken from this river isn't meant to be eaten." He taught me that we must learn what to keep, what to let go of, or throw back. He taught life's lessons the same way he taught me how to cast my rod, and he taught me well.

This is the part of my life that I desire to share with you—not only the stories of my career as a Harlem Globetrotter, but how my life lessons made me a better person for the universe. In this book, I will give you those bits of wisdom called Hallieisms that were taught to me by my father, family, and many other influential people in my life. I have gone to the well many times and have taken that wisdom which is instrumental in propelling me to great levels of success which I define as fearlessness, inner harmony, and abundance. These principles and Hallieisms can do the same, or even more, for you if you receive them with an open-mind and internalize them with your heart. For you to reap full benefit from these rich universal truths, you must make them a part of your *thinking, feeling, action,* and *re-action* (TFAR). **YES!**™ The key here is sincere receptivity and to realize that accurate repetition makes the mastery. Repetition is the mother of skill development. Proper repetition allowed me to perfect the Finger Spin as illustrated in Photograph E.

Hallie demonstrates an accomplished skill known as the "Finger Spin." He says that if you practice and repeat an exercise often enough, true mastery is possible.

Photograph E

"Take your head out from under the sand. Everyday is born anew, and every minute is a new beginning—So take a minute and make new value-added choices."

Hallie Bryant and Robert Frost

INTRODUCTION

Life is Not *One* Slam Dunk

"Life is not a horrible problem to be solved,
life is a wonderful game to be played:
A game called Life."

HALLIE BRYANT

Just as in the game of basketball, there are ground rules that govern life's actions. It is impossible to have harmony with anyone else without having harmony with self first. From time to time we will take a one-minute break to review a "TIMEOUT" card.

The Ground Rules are listed on the next page and are outlined in TIMEOUT #1. Rule #1 is very important and it is to help you get the most from this book. To achieve this mission, you must be willing to make a **Willingness Power Agreement** with yourself. The Willingness Power Agreement is a promise that you make to yourself. It is a commitment to read and study the material in this book with an open-mind and to refrain from pre-judging the material to give yourself the

TIMEOUT #1

The Willingness Power Agreement
The Ground Rules

1. You must be willing to make a willingness power agreement with yourself. The Willingness Power Agreement is to read and study this material with an open-mind and refrain from pre-judging the material to give yourself the opportunity to view this information from a different perspective.

2. Let us not repeat history by thinking from a confused mind instead of a mature mind. The confused mind is scattered and fragmented. It is disharmonious. The mature mind is focused and in harmony. It has positive energy and a firm foundation.

3. Recognize and understand the value of making a paradigm shift. Make every effort not to slip back into old modes by taking life for granted.

4. As we begin this journey, in all that you do first seek understanding not just intellectual memory.

opportunity to view this information from various perspectives."

If we expect honesty and integrity from others, we must be willing to *be* honest and *have* integrity. As a matter of fact, we should be willing to be all of those things that we desire from others. We attract what we are. Review the Willingness Power Agreement often to help you keep an open-mind during this journey. Your efforts will reward you. **YES!**™

Oftentimes we are our own saboteurs. We get in our own way and become our own enemies. We have two natures, paradoxically, our Higher Self, which is also known as the true self and the "Lower Self," which is also known as the false self. The true self is in harmony with the universal positive energy. Also known as "The Big Me," it is that part of us that is connected with and a part of our divine Creator. The false self thrives on negativity and in being out of balance or disharmony. Our lower self is negative and has a fearful ego. The false self is also known as "The Little Me."

Even though the false self is "The Little Me," it will fight ferociously to keep its territory. We allow "The Little Me" to lead. We attempt to improve our life, or begin a new project, or relationship with the *grand finale*. In basketball, we call this maneuver, the awesome, in your face **slam-dunk.** It is an attention grabber, everyone gets excited, and it is a temporary ego booster. The problem is that it raises the bar and the expectations of others and it creates a mindset of expecting something greater, especially if it is early in the game. The slam-dunk works on the court, particularly if it is the last basket of the game. However in life, if you begin with the slam-dunk, where do you go from there? Where is the strong foundation? In some instances, it is all downhill from there.

As human beings, we love the excitement created by anticipation. We enjoy the thrill of the hunt and the pleasures of the unknown. Too often, the potential excitement, the thrill or mystery is extinguished before these desires have had the opportunity to ignite the spirit or build a firm foundation. Some of the premature slam-dunks that we engage in are sex before the relationship, the $50,000 sports car as a graduation gift to the high school graduate, and multi-million dollar contracts before proof of performance and maturity. We believe that in many ways some of these pre-mature slam-dunks contribute to high divorce rates, young people not feeling the need to be responsible and giving them a sense of entitlement. Pre-mature slam-dunks also may contribute to millionaire hoodlums and substance abusers. It is no surprise that some may lose interest in what they are achieving so quickly and may be willing to blow it all in a non-thinking moment. Remember, excitement vanishes quickly—wisdom lingers. Pre-mature slam-dunks may be CODE blockers. Life is a process and ignoring the CODE interrupts that process, causing negative things to occur. **YES!**™

The rules and process to follow in order to have balance leads to *harmony*. Harmony is established when you get your PEMSS—the Physical, Emotional, Mental, Spiritual, and Social self in accord or proper balance. We must understand that acquiring balance is a process that allows for many mini-slam-dunks occurring along the way. Therefore, you will have those moments of ecstasy and elation. The difference is that you will have more of them.

The Harlem Globetrotters travel around the world inspiring and entertaining audiences from all walks of life. During my day we performed for children and adults of all ages including the military, celebrities, and royalty. Photograph F is a picture of us with comedian Red Skelton.

A team is composed of individuals with various backgrounds and life experiences and that is true for the Harlem Globetrotters. A team brings various attitudes, systems, beliefs and values to the court. In order for a team to play at its best, which is at its full potential, the team members must get their minds and ac-

Pictured from L to R: Jumping Jackie Jackson, Screaming Mel Davis,
Red Skelton, Meadowlark Lemon, and Hallie Bryant.
Kneeling is Fred "Curly" Neal

Photograph F

tions synchronized to play in a unique rhythm that works for no one else but themselves. This type of rhythm is what we refer to as harmony. My teams, whether it was in high school, college, or the Globetrotters, had harmony—as sweet as the tune "Sweet Georgia Brown."

Harmony is what each of you need to establish for yourself so that the mind, body and soul can work collectively together. This union is known as the Hallieism called **PEMSS** (The Physical, Emotional, Mental, Spiritual, and Social) self. If you do not have your PEMSS working together, you keep tripping over yourself, like the players do when they are out of sync with each other. In my opinion, no one individual personified harmony for the Globetrotters like Reese "Goose" Tatum. He was entertaining in all that he did including walking, talking, acting, socializing, working, and playing.

Take a look at Exhibit 1, Hallie's Wheel of Harmony, which is symbolic of an old-fashioned wagon wheel. The hub or center is the heart of the individual or organization. The spokes are the workers, team members, employees, or family members. The rim is the company, the family, or body of the organization or group. The rim forms a circle—a unity circle. It takes all of the parts working together for efficiency and effectiveness. This forms an environment fostering harmonious relationships. When all of the parts are working harmoniously the whole is greater than the sum of its parts. **YES!**™

I use this exercise in a segment called "Hallie's Wheel of Harmony." This physically interactive activity eases the participant's inhibitions and they discover their hidden talents. Remember, the lack of fun can cause premature aging. It has been experience that participants leave my sessions feeling energized and more in harmony with themselves.

It is my opinion that the magnificent Chicago Bulls of the late eighties and early nineties, informally known as the "Michael Jordan and Phil Jackson Era," by many,

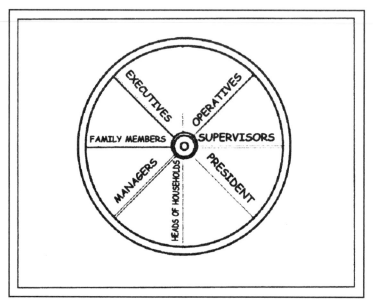

Exhibit 1

HALLIE'S WHEEL OF HARMONY™

The hub or center is the heart of the individual or organization. The spokes are the workers, team members, employees, or family members. The rim is the company, the family, or body of the organization or group. The rim forms a circle—a unity circle. It takes all of the parts working together for efficiency and effectiveness.

was no mistake. Their harmony could be witnessed almost every time they showed up to play. I believe that basketball geniuses such as Julius "Dr. J" Erving, Oscar

"The Big O" Robertson, Earvin "Magic" Johnson, Larry Bird, and Bob Cousy had a special rhythm when they played. If you have never witnessed a player who passes a ball to his or her teammate without first checking to see if the teammate is there, then you are missing a beautiful moment. Successful teams create a harmony that allows them to win and sustain an almost unreal level of unconscious competence—a level of mastery that allows them to move without thought. Magic Johnson epitomized those passing skills on the basketball court. I am sure that the Harlem Globetrotter's style of play influenced Magic's total game. You need to create this inner harmony or rhythm for yourself.

The key principle to focus on is the **habit.** What the eyes see and the ears hear, if seen and heard often enough, will be remembered and become a part of us. Repetition creates the habit and will be discussed in chapter twelve. With your PEMSS and habits in check, you are equipped to break the CODE.

Life is about the *co-ordination* of our efforts, the *organization* of our thoughts, the *direction* that our thinking takes us, and the *energy* expended to manifest our desires. As we bring the aforementioned four areas together in harmony with our habits, we break the CODE.

Then, it is revealed to us what we need to create

harmony in our lives. But first, we must take a few steps back and evaluate where we were, appreciate where we are, and understand that *all that we desire to become is possible if we focus on breaking the CODE*

TIMEOUT #2

THE CODE is the overall effect that the Coordination, Organization, Direction, and Energy of purposeful thinking have on well developed habits. Proper balance of these factors will lead to harmony. With harmony, all things are possible.

Harmony is the working together of the PEMSS (Physical, Emotional, Mental, Spiritual, and Social) self.

A Habit is the repetition of a behavior until it is a learned behavior and is done unconsciously.

The True Self is "The Big Me" or Higher Self

The False Self is "The Little Me" or Lower Self

RBMG- Relax Breathe and Move Gracefully

WOW—Well of Wisdom

CODE

COORDINATION

Section I   COORDINATION

Triangle of Harmony—The Triangle Offense

> *"Coordination is the harmonious or effective working together of different parts: the arrangements of parts into an effective relation."*
>
> THE CONCISE OXFORD ENGLISH DICTIONARY

OVERVIEW

We program our minds for success. It is for us to determine whether or not we are going to make our behavior useful or useless. Anybody worth anything should be able to be used. There is nothing wrong with being used properly. That really means that you have value. The slight distinction is whether you are being used or misused. God grant me the wisdom to know the difference.

To take control of your life you must take a purposeful offensive approach. This type of aggressive approach will allow you to maximize your potential. When you function with purpose, you increase your chances of adding value to what you do and not being misused. Purposeful living gives you the opportunity to make regular assessments of your habits. Your habits form useful or useless skills. A skill is an accumulation of habits coordinated together, to perform a task.

You operate out of your habits. Habits are those repeated learned behaviors that allow you to function at the level of unconscious competence. If you have a habit that needs to be changed or done away with all together, you will find that it will be difficult to give up. Initially, you may not change the habit but you can modify it. We will explore the impact that habits have on the coordination of the Triangle Offense—Self-discipline, Courage, and Persistence as illustrated in Exhibit 2.

In most major sports be it hockey, baseball, or basketball there is a triangle offense. As a matter of fact, there is a triangle offense for entrepreneurs. Phil Jackson led the Bulls to six championships in eight years. When he became coach of the Los Angeles Lakers he carried his version of the triangle offense with him. "We're trying to get across to the players how much awareness it takes all the time to be part of this team," Jackson said. "You've got to constantly be aware of what you're doing, you don't just go through the motions." It did not take long for the Lakers to get in harmony and capture a third championship.

As the architect of your success, you must build your own triangle offense one side at a time. Start with *Self-discipline* as discussed in Chapter One because it is the foundation of the triangle. Remember, self-discipline is not self-punishment. It is self-growth and self-mastery. How well you develop in the area of self-discipline will determine your successful outcomes. Chapter Two will be a discussion on Courage, and Chapter Three on Persistence.

Exhibit 2

TRIANGLE OF HARMONY

CHAPTER ONE

"The birth of every action is a thought."

HALLIE BRYANT

SELF-DISCIPLINE

Self-discipline is an uncoiling of four related terms: *thoughts, feelings, actions,* and *results* (TFAR) leading to consequences. Exhibit 3 illustrates this uncoiling. At the center of self-discipline is thought. Nothing happens without a thought. The ancestor of every action is a thought.

As thoughts unfold, feelings evolve. Feelings are unleashed energy and feelings need managing. Your actions are behaviors that surface when you feel. We must understand that for every action there are consequences and these consequences are the results of the action. We ask ourselves what are the many forces that guide us and make us behave in such a manner?

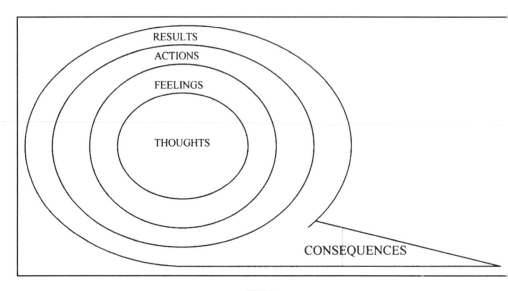

TFAR

EXHIBIT 3

The Uncoiling of Self-discipline

Regardless of who speaks of these forces, they may be presented in various formats. Og Mandino, the author of *The Greatest Secret in the World,* acknowledges that these forces are *Appetite, Passion, Prejudice, Greed, Love, Fear, Environment,* and *Habit.*

Appetite: We get hungry for whatever need presents itself. Examples of these needs are physiological such as shelter, safety, social interaction, esteem, and self-actualization. Higher needs cannot adequately be satisfied until the more base needs are met. We need completion and satisfaction of those lower or base needs before moving forward.

If you do not manage your appetite, your appetite will manage you. It can become deadly in that it can get out of control. That is why self-discipline is so important in the growth and development process. Tame and train all these forces. It does not matter whether or not it is an appetite for food, sex, or money.

Passion: A deep desire for something or someone. Passion is a strong, barely controllable emotion. Nothing is good or bad except thinking makes it so. When you are ignorant and using passion as the motive to act, the consequences may mean the accidental death of another.

For instance, you are inside your home. You hear what sounds like an awful collision. You look outside and see that a car collided with a truck. A man is lying on the sidewalk with trauma to his head. You start feeling sorry for him. You lift him up to help him not realizing that he has a broken neck. You were driven to do something and without thinking first, you moved him. Unless you are extremely skilled in this area, what you should have done was to get help, cover him up, and keep him warm until the professionals arrive. So you have to manage your passion. Anything carried to extreme may be detrimental to yourself and others.

Prejudice: We all have prejudices. We all prejudge. Let us not confuse bigotry with prejudice because that is something different. Bigotry is the same as hate which springs from fear, insecurity, and ignorance. The purpose of bigotry is to divide and conquer for selfish reasons.

If we judge, especially without facts, and do not even know that we are doing it, then we are using conditioned thoughts that may be inaccurate. Many of our actions are unconscious and we are not aware of their influence. Judging without facts is often a learned behavior resulting in blindness. Prejudging is action based on subjective and unwarranted fears. It is also a conditioned response or an emotional reaction similar to a knee-jerk reaction.

Greed: Greed gives us drive to do things. It is an intense or excessive desire. However we must emphasize that anything carried to extreme not only can be, but will be, a detriment.

Love: It is said that "love is a many-splendored thing," and "love is the way I walk in gratitude." Love is never lost. If not reciprocated, it will flow back, soften and purify the heart.

However, love without awareness is detrimental. When love is in balance with productive and useful energy, it creates a state of tranquility and harmony; an attitude of abundance versus scarcity.

Fear: Fear is energy running rampant. A common acronym for fear is *False Energy Appearing Real*. I extend that acronym to FEAR to focus on Feeling, Energy, Awareness, and Replacement.

Environment: What you are around you learn.
What you learn you practice.
What you practice you become, and
What you become has consequences.

Habit: A learned behavior. We are creatures of habit.
Sow your thoughts and your sowing reaps an action.
Sow an action and reap a habit.
Sow a habit and reap a character.
Sow a character and reap a destiny.

Awareness is the key to all of these forces and helps us to tame and train them. To know better is not sufficient to do better. You will only do better when your awareness expands. Truth is a perception—yours or mine. Reality is what is happening right now. Awareness is the spotlight to reality.

TIMEOUT #3

Self-discipline is the foundation of the triangle.

It is an uncoiling of thoughts at the center, feelings, actions, and results all leading to consequences.

The forces that guide us are appetite, passion, prejudice, greed, love, fear, environment, and habit.

The awareness is key to tame and train all forces.

You will only do better when your awareness expands.

Chapter Two

COURAGE

Courage is not a lack of fear, but the ability to face fear instead of fleeing from it. Fear is energy running rampant and it is an emotion that needs to be tamed. Courage will surface when you begin to think clearly. Awareness of the fear is the first step. Decide if it is a warranted or unwarranted fear. Once you begin to deal with this fear it will move you from the fear-frozen position or belief to action.

What you face and acknowledge you can better control or manage. Remember, what you refuse to face and acknowledge can control you. Are you the puppet or the puppeteer? You have a choice. You can either live by chance or by choice. Just do not confuse the two.

It is natural for you to travel the path of least resistance. This path is the most comfortable and does not take you out of your comfort zone. To create different results for yourself sometimes you must take calculated risks. Understand that jumping off a mountain is not being a risk taker. If you jump off the mountain you can "bet the farm" what the outcome will be. A risk is something that you may engage in and not be certain of the outcome. That is why you should take a calculated risk. First, reasonably evaluate the situation. Second , draw parameters around the challenge to determine what you are willing and not willing to do, and finally—after you have considered all of the factors that you are aware of that may influence the outcome-ACT.

This process which erases fear and replaces it with courage gives you the comfort level you need to be free to move forward. With freedom comes responsibility, but it is not without risk. It takes courage! Basically, you erase and replace. This is a major paradigm shift.

Chapter Three

> *"A wise man (or woman) will make
> more opportunities than he (or she) will find."*
>
> Sir Frances Bacon

PERSISTENCE

It was exciting to snag my first fish. It was persistence that enabled me to land it. Persistence is a lesson in endurance. Persistence is continuously turning the page of "stickability". It is knowing that "giving up" is not an option.

As a Globetrotter I had to practice moves and develop skills that were not customarily accomplished by the best professional NBA players. Former Globetrotters Marques Haynes and Curly Neal exhibited great ball-handling skills. They could dribble the basketball better than anyone. To the viewer their ball-handling was nothing short of miraculous. However, the techniques became second nature to us. Through repetition we tried and tried until we achieved the maneuver. Then we moved on to the next challenging maneuver until we had perfected it. After learning basics, we were able to combine the maneuvers and turn them into highly skillful routines. As it is said, "inch by inch it is a cinch but by the yard it is hard."

The best way not to lose focus of a goal is to break it down into smaller parts. The key to achieving big action is little action. Master the smaller parts and move to the next level. This way you can record the small successes and build to the slam-dunks. "A minute's success pays for the failure of years."

I do not want to be deceptive. Persistence takes a lot of energy and focus. Balance keeps you in harmony. It is important to have the "3Fs and B"—*focus, flow, flex, and balance.* Focus is staying centered with clarity and awareness. Flow to get into the silent rhythm of the situation and be flexible enough to go with the flow and maintain balance which produces harmony. YES!™ Focus is concentrated and well-directed energy. To flow shows stability. When you function with little or no turbulence, your coordination flows as smooth as silk. Many smooth basketball players receive nicknames such as silk. When you are non-stagnant, you are like a river or current of air that can transport you to your destiny. Flex or flexibility is the ability to adapt and to think outside the box when necessary so as not to get locked in to any negative energy.

It helps to possess the "3 Fs and B" when you are young. When you have little control over your circumstances, it is best to remain focused and flexible enough to go with the flow. My family and I moved to Indianapolis when I was about nine years old. I attended Public School #17. There I met the influential coach that would change my life forever. That man was Mr. Ray Crowe. He was not only my Junior High School coach but my high school coach as well. At Crispus Attucks High School he coached world-renown players such as "The Big O" Oscar Robertson, shown in photo H, and "Wee" Willie Gardner. We affectionately addressed our coach as either Mr. Crowe or Coach Crowe, but was lovingly called "The Razor" in small huddles. Mr. Crowe was razor sharp in his speech, appearance, and skills. As far as I am concerned, Coach Crowe epitomized the Fabulous Four—Firm, Fair, Flexible, and Frank. Mr. Crowe was my role model and I wanted to be just like him. Mr. Crowe is pictured in Photograph G.

The Fabulous Four, more commonly known as *firm, fair, flexible,* and *frank,* is not a singing group from the seventies. The Fabulous Four is a group of tools that

work in concert with each other for you to use to pre-
pare yourself for success. It is important to be as firm
with yourself as you are with others. You must realize
that time is a limited component of your success formula. Be firm enough to let others know how you wish
to be treated. Be fair and treat others as you wish to be
treated. You attract to you what you are. The best plans

Coach Ray Crowe

Photograph G

TIMEOUT #4

"A minute's success pays for the failure of years."

Robert Browning

Focus Flow and Flex combined with Balance

Inch by Inch it's a cinch
By the Yard it's hard.

Master the smaller parts then move up to the next level.

can be thwarted. Inasmuch as you can exercise control over yourself, there are some things that you cannot control. Be flexible and allow for adjustments. Firm and frank are dependent tools because one depends on the other when communicating effectively. Firm is how you will hold fast to your decisions and frank is how strong and articulate you will be when directing your responses, orders, or information.

"The Big O" Oscar Robertson and Hallie Bryant

Photograph H

C
O

ORGANIZATION

D
E

Section II   ORGANIZATION

What's In It for Me?

> *"All the good the past has had—*
> *remains to make your own time glad!"*
>
> Dr. Venice Bloodworth

OVERVIEW

Organization is your ability to throw nine balls in the air and keep them simultaneously bouncing, moving, or spinning until you have placed each one of them in their final expected resting place. Is that a challenge? You bet it is! Even more challenging is to know that two or three more balls will be tossed at you expecting the same successful outcome.

Make a note to remind yourself that this information is cumulative. What you learn in previous chapters is to be meshed with new information. Organization is being able to bring your affairs or business into order. Part of achieving this feat focuses on self-discipline. Add courage and persistence to self-discipline you will find yourself reading Chapter Four—The Power of Purpose, Chapter Five—Passion Will Allow You to Soar, and Chapter Six—Vision: By Focusing, You Will See It, and Come to Know.

Chapter Four

"Consciousness of our powers augment them."

VAUVENARGUES

THE POWER OF PURPOSE

Discovering your purpose is a private affair. You must look within to find your purpose. Talking to others will allow you to know how they feel about you, but only you can decide what makes you happy. Only you will know what makes you look forward to the next day and make life worth living.

Identifying your purpose is a project. When you go under construction, initially, it should be a private affair. Man can change his total self by changing the attitude of his mind. It is noted that as early as the year 1900 William James, a Harvard Professor, who is considered the father of American psychology, said that you can change who you are by changing what goes into your mind. Up until 1900 the majority of the people who studied behavior did not think you could change behavior. Prior to that time most researchers thought that genetics determined who you are. So you can change what you are and who you are by the choices you make. You want to program what you desire to enter your thought process, your consciousness. One of the greatest tools to get us to that stage (as espoused by Ernie Larsen) is our ERSCHB (*Execution, Repetition, Successes, Confidence, Habit, and Belief*) System. This system refers to the programming in place and the reprogramming necessary to effectuate change. Repetition is the mother of skill development. Examine your programming by examining your beliefs. Chapter Fifteen will cover this system in more detail. Another Hallieism is PBAFAR—Programming, Beliefs, Attitude, Feelings, Action, and Results. Part of this model is summarized in Exhibit 4.

Others will want to contribute to your personal development. Ignore them for the time being to avoid mix messages and confused data. Here you are avoiding the confused mind and are feeding it with what you want to come out of it. You have your own method and trust in the process. Discover your purpose and watch your energy level soar.

CHAPTER FIVE

"I want to be thoroughly used up when I die,
for the harder I work, the more I live.
Life is no brief candle for me. It is a sort
of splendid torch which I have got hold of
for a moment, and I want to make it
burn as brightly as possible before
handing it to future generations."

GEORGE BERNARD SHAW

PASSION WILL ALLOW
YOUR MIND TO SOAR

Floating in the air before Michael Jordan were Hallie "The Comet" Bryant along with many other legends such as, Walt Frazier, Julius "Dr. J" Erving, Bob Pettit, Oscar the "Big O" Robertson, and Bill Walton. I could hear and feel their passion about the game just listening to them in an interview. When they speak about the game, you know that it is almost an uncontrollable outpouring of emotion.

In the early days, I recall how much I loved the game. Passion is sitting in a hot crowded bus with other teammates for several days at a time and knowing that this is as good as it gets. Passion is desiring to still play the game for the same people who cheered and applauded your performance as an athlete on the court but prohibited you from eating in the dining area reserved for "whites only" which I viewed as an opportunity to teach. Passion is having the opportunity to play the game you love regardless of the circumstances. If you "really" desire to find harmony, find your lifes passion and you too will soar and PUUR through life. YES!™

"PUUR"

If you really desire to find harmony, find your lifes passion and you too will soar and PUUR through life. YES!™

Purposeful

Useful

Understandable

Relevant

Chapter Six

VISION BY FOCUSING, YOU WILL SEE IT, AND COME TO KNOW

You have to have freedom of thinking to have vision. As stated by Guy Finley, the author of *The Secret of Letting Go*, "Never believe that the limits of your present view are the limits of your possibility." The degree to which you will awaken will be in direct proportion to the amount of truth that you can accept about yourself. As the master teacher says, "It is the truth that will set you free." However, you cannot escape prison until you recognize you are in one. Awareness first—**YES!**™

There are two kinds of freedom—authentic freedom and counterfeit freedom. Authentic freedom is real. One must pay the price to get the reward. Counterfeit freedom is short term gain and may result in long term pain. Sometimes we seek this kind of freedom when we overindulge in gambling, drinking, alcohol, and other substance abuse activities. Instead of seeking relief from our inner pain by engaging in the above behaviors, we should be engaged in the process called MUFIT—*Mercy, Understanding, Forgiveness, Imagination, and Truth.* Mercy is a form of useful empathy. Understanding is a clear insight—seeing the big picture. Forgiveness of self first is one of the toughest things to do, but must be done. Imagination is *imagineering* which is described as tweaking the thoughts being recreated—a re-framing. Truth is reality and it will not go away, therefore it must be confronted and dealt with accordingly. The truth may not always be the way we want it but it is the reality of the situation. It is the only thing that will set you free. YES!™

The reality or truth for African-Americans in the early part of the twentieth century was that the male athletes had little opportunity to play professional sports. Abe Saperstein, the founder of the original Harlem Globetrotters pictured in Photograph I, was a great visionary, innovator, mentor, and friend.

He saw an opportunity to change the reality of basketball and afforded great athletes the opportunity to showcase their talents. He did not like the situation, so

ABE SAPERSTEIN – Owner, Harlem Globetrotters Basketball Team

Abe Saperstein

Photograph I

he re-framed it. By a stroke of luck and great timing, Abe Saperstein was introduced to a super-talented basketball player. Saperstein could envision Reese Tatum as a multi-faceted athlete. Immediately, Saperstein could see him as the Harlem Globetrotter's "King of

Reese "Goose" Tatum

Photograph J

Comedy." Reese Tatum was known worldwide as Goose Tatum. Goose is pictured in Photograph J.

I observed Saperstein in all that he said and did. He treated me fairly and he allowed me to do my original one-man Harlem Globetrotter Show during the off-season. This was a win-win situation. I learned volumes through my association with Abe by observing him operate the organization.

It is a challenge to make the paradigm shift from thinking with CODE blockers that inhibits the ability to think outside the box to thinking freely. To get a better vision for yourself and to assist you in making paradigm shifts, go back and review the information in Chapter Three under *Discipline* concerning thoughts, feelings, actions, and results. When you give yourself permission to dream and create the desire to act on your vision, understand that a Hallieism that helped me as well as Abe was the ability to under stand A-T & T.

Ask yourself three questions: "Is what I want to do or say APPROPRIATE? Is it TIMELY? Is it TASTEFUL?" If it does not hurt you, or anyone else, or the Universe, you may just have a winning idea or plan.

TIMEOUT #5

However, you cannot escape prison until you recognize you are in one. Awareness first—YES!™

Discover your purpose and you will find your passion

The Purpose of thinking Big, someone said, I bargained in life for a penny, and Life would pay no more.

A -T and T   An action should be Appropriate, Timely and Tasteful

A recommended book *Doing What You Love and Loving What You Do* by Robert Anthony.

CODE

DIRECTION

E

Section III DIRECTION

It's Your RNA Not Your DNA that Determines Your Success

> *"I think that one of the most important lessons to learn is that we are all responsible for our lives. But nobody gets through this life alone. Everybody needs somebody to show them a way out, or a way up. Everybody does."*
>
> OPRAH WINFREY

OVERVIEW

The greatest barrier to self-improvement is saying and believing the statement, "I already knew that." When a person makes that statement, he closes his mind to everything that comes afterwards. Even if the information is something that he had heard before, it would be better to say that "this sounds familiar", and listen for deeper understanding from a fresh perspective. Even if he knows that he has heard it before, he is at a different place and has experienced new things. Life is always in a state of flux. One may have a different view on old information. "When I was a child, I spoke as a child, I understood as a child, I thought as a child: but when I became a man, I put away childish things," (I)Corinthians 13:11. I take time to process and reflect as part of my daily routine. I am pictured in Photograph K in my

"Talk to yourself and know that it is your RNA that will lead you to a successful and harmonious life."

Photograph K

office taking that moment to think about how my RNA has gotten me to this place.

When a person thinks that genetics has him stuck, there is no room for growth. Success is not determined by your DNA but your RNA.

We have heard a lot about *deoxyribonucleic acid* or what is commonly known as "DNA". DNA is the code of life that has been misleading to some people. DNA is a self-replicating material which is present in nearly all living organisms and is the carrier of genetic information. When so-called friends and even sometimes well-meaning family members want to put you down, oftentimes they make comments as if you are genetically coded for failure. They have said demeaning phrases like "you are no good" and "you are worthless." Like a tape recorder, these demeaning phrases and the following "put downs" play in the minds of many individuals who are trying to prove the family and friends wrong. You, too, may have heard many of these. Listed are a few reminders in the *List of Common Putdowns.*

Negative words are harsh and will eat at your core. Take a moment here and enjoy taking a pen or marker and place a huge "X" across the putdown list and say, "Cancel, cancel." If this is not your reality, it is the reality of too many individuals. The power of your crossing out this chart will remind you not to be a giver or

LIST OF COMMON PUT DOWNS

- You're just like your father (inferring that your father was an irresponsible bum).
- Your mother was no good and you are going to be just like her, you *harlot*!
- You're stupid, your mother is stupid and your daddy is stupid. You don't have a chance to be anything other than what you are, a stupid person.
- Who do you think you are?

receiver of such vile language. This is all of the energy that should be expended with dealing with other people's opinion of you. Now RBMG, relax, breathe, and move gracefully to the next paragraph.

As disturbing as this language is, if you don't understand anything else in this book, you must understand that, the concept espoused by Vernon Howard, one of my favorite authors, is that it is not your DNA that will determine your success, it is the RNA—your ability to

Rise above your usual thinking.
Never fear your own confusion;
All answers are discovered within.

Let's not confuse this RNA with *Ribonucleic Acid,* the primary agent of protein formation that processes genetic information from DNA molecules into enzymes necessary for life. The RNA we will be talking about in this section is your ability to **Rise** above your usual thinking by making that paradigm shift. **Neve**r fear your own confusion and make sure you are operating from a mature mind. ***All*** answers are discovered within. The divineness is in each of us. Choose to cultivate it.

To move forward, it is required of us to RISE above our usual thinking. Many times our usual thinking is what has landed us where we are today. At first it is uncomfortable when we begin to think differently. When we begin to think differently, we behave differently and have to reset our comfort zone.

NEVER fear your own confusion. Confusion is compared to a muddy lake or mud-hole. If you have fresh water coming through that muddy lake it will eventually clear up. If it just stays there without fresh water coming in, it just remains a mud-hole infested with mosquitoes, and it allows everything to take from it until it dries up and is never recognized as a lake again. If new value-adding thoughts are not constantly flowing through a receptive or mature mind, it will dry up just like the muddy lake. That is when you have heard people say things like you do not seem like yourself. Your brain sends messages to you that sounds something like this:

SIGNS OF A STAGNANT MIND

Nobody likes me.

I'm bored.

I need a change.

Life is meaningless.

I need some excitement.

By pumping fresh useful thoughts into your mind, you allow it to renew and refresh itself and get off of stuck or a "fear-frozen" mind. Time must be allowed for change to occur. You must give yourself the opportunity to adjust to the different ways of thinking or doing things. Be patient with yourself as you move from the confused mind into the mature mind. New behavior and thoughts have to be reinforced by repetition until the new behavior becomes a habit.

ALL answers are discovered within. In fact, confusion many times is necessary before clarity can come. Allow for your natural unfolding. Energy is flowing through and around each of us. We just have to learn how to recognize and tap into this energy. Just like one apple has enough seeds to produce bushels of apples, one thought, especially the correct thought, can produce more positive outcomes than we could have imagined. You will discover that you can change your

---

TIMEOUT #6

Rise above your usual thinking.
Never fear your own confusion;
All answers are discovered within.

Pump new useful thoughts into the confused mind and move gracefully into the mature mind.

The mind, like a lake, will dry up if it is not allowed to refresh itself with new thoughts.

Choose and manage your thoughts and you manage your life.

present circumstances in Chapter Seven—Learn From the Past, Plan for the Future, Live in the Now (LPL). In Chapter Eight—Beliefs, Values, Assumptions, and Memories (BVAMs) you will identify those factors that determine your present behavior.

Chapter Seven

"I always remember that I have everything I need to enjoy my here and now—unless I am letting my consciousness be dominated by demands and expectations— based on the dead past or the imagined future."

Ken Keyes

LEARN FROM THE PAST, PLAN FOR THE FUTURE, LIVE IN THE NOW (LPL)

My trusted and loyal childhood companion was my dog, *I Know*. Now I know, that *I Know* is a strange name for a dog, at that time, for some reason it just seemed appropriate to name him *I Know*. Before I got my dog I spent a lot of time around older kids and adults. The only thing my tender ears could understand from their conversations was the fact that every time they began to have a conversation, the other person would always say "I know" or "I already knew that." Well, when I got my dog, and he was a smart dog, I named him *I Know*.

I Know and I had many wonderful years together. To let him go was difficult when he had to be put to sleep. Papa taught me how to let go, lighten up, and let God. It was most difficult! The lesson here was not to be too attached to anything because he did not belong to me anyway. I learned that that which is given to you will be returned from whence it came, the Creator.

HE WHO KNOWS . . .

He who knows and knows that he knows is a wise person—follow him

He who knows and knows not they he knows is asleep—wake him

He who knows not and knows that he knows not is simple—teach him

He that knows not and knows not that he knows not is a fool—shun him.

An Arabian Proverb

As you can see from the above, sip from the well of wisdom, you do not want to be known as "He (she) who knows not and knows not that he (she) knows not". A fool has a closed mind. You do not need to have a hole in your head to have an open mind. Lighten up! **YES!**™

When others recognize you as a closed-minded individual, they have a tendency of viewing you as a weed. They pluck you from their environment so as not to give you multiplying power.

We will discuss in Chapter Ten that we are a miniature Universe and that we are constantly cultivating our garden. We must protect what we plant in our mental garden to reap a healthy harvest.

There is so much negativity around us that it is so easy to doubt ourselves. Friends, family, the media, and others, for many reasons, are compelled to constantly remind us of our past failures, slowly tearing down our defense mechanisms and shifting the mind back to the old ways of thinking and processing information . Just knowing better will not sustain us. We have to constantly plan for the future. We need to use our faith to guard against the critics or so-called supporters. It is imperative that we believe in ourselves. That is how we maintain our new mindset.

Always keep the "Big Picture" in mind. Your present condition probably will not be your future. Even if you try to stay exactly where you are, there are too many uncontrollable factors that can change your financial, physical, and/or mental conditions. You invest wisely, only to discover that a major company in your portfolio went "belly-up". You open your mail and a white powdery substance falls from the envelope. Finally, after much searching, you encounter the love of your life and he or she discovers that they have cancer. Does that mean that you should give up on planning and having a positive outlook? No! Plan for the future. You control more than you know, but always keep the "Big Picture" in mind and live in the now.

THE BIG PICTURE

Resolve to be

    Compassionate with the aged

    Tender with the young

    Sympathetic with the striving and

    Tolerant with the weak and the wrong.

For someday in our lives we will have been all of the above.

                      Author Unknown

It is much more difficult to hit a moving target, so always be actively engaged in changing your environment for yourself or for someone else. You can never give out more than you will receive. Because you control so much that happens to you, make the most out of it. I heard Earl Nightingale quote a philosopher about progressive realization of a worthy idea. Mr. Nightingale said, "We become what we think about." One of my favorite philosophers, Henry David Thoreau, commented that, "if one advances confidently in the direction of his own dream and endeavors to live a life which he has imagined, he will meet with success unexpected in common hours . . . following his beliefs."

THREE CRITERIA FOR DOING

What Is Right

Will it hurt someone else?

Will it hurt me?

Will it hurt the Universe?

If not so, go for it and self- correct where needed.

Make peace with imperfection.

MPWI: Make Peace With Imperfection. **YES!**™

In following your beliefs, I believe there are three criteria for doing what is right. Will it hurt someone else, will it hurt me, will it hurt the Universe? If not, go forward and self-correct if necessary. Remember "A-T&T" and make peace with imperfection (MPWI).

Chapter Eight

"Old beliefs will not lead you to new opportunities."

O'Merrial Butchee

BELIEFS, VALUES, ASSUMPTIONS, AND MEMORIES (BVAMS)

It often has been said that, 1) what you are around you learn, 2) what you learn you practice, 3) what you practice you become, 4) and what you become has consequences. Your subconscious does not care what you tell it. Whatever you tell yourself, if you say it often enough, it will evolve into your self-talk. What you feed your mind will either build you up or it will pull you down. If you do not believe in it, it will not work for you. **YES!**™

You cannot escape those mental tapes that are playing in your head. Like a muscle, belief increases with use. The key to checking and assessing *your Beliefs, Values, Assumptions,* and *Memories* (BVAMs) is to become aware of or increase your awareness of those tapes that are shaping your thinking. Not until then will you have some idea of how to replant your mental garden.

Many times our environment sets the tone for how we are to live and what influences our belief and value systems. This environment will impact our decision making processes, so we are to be selective as to the choices we make. Our actions create memories and by responding, the same way, to similar situations repeatedly, our BVAMs become deeply-rooted. This continuous repetition of functioning from our BVAMs creates our mental framework and our mental framework dictates our reality.

1. Does good exist in your BVAMs?
2. Is there any misinformation in your BVAMs?

We believe that the answer to question 1 is "yes" and our response to question 2 is "more than likely." As a matter of fact, all of us are carrying around plenty of unconscious misinformation. Sometimes it is not until we run into the truth and it is revealed to us beyond reasonable doubt that we will purge our mind from this misinformation.

Changing the way we view things is one of the most difficult paradigm shifts to make. We have spent years, sometimes decades, believing and acting a certain way based on assumptions that the information in our minds is accurate. Know that we are not alone and that true success and harmony are more achievable when we are being ourselves. To say, "To be free I have to be me" is to claim our birthright. To be "OK" with our present condition causes us to know that we have the ability to change it by using the tools presented in this book.

This information can be as true and clear as rain water, and it can improve lives, but if you don't believe it, it will not work for you. The law of life is the law of belief. When you have belief, you must use it. Belief, like any other habit, increases with use.

Belief eases you into FAITH—not FATE. Fate is believing that you cannot do anything about a situation. Fate is a power regarded as predetermining events unalterable. It is written in the Bible, "Now faith is the substance of things hoped for, the evidence of things not seen" Hebrews 11:1. Remember, you are never alone when you have FAITH.

FAITH is:

Father
And
I
Together
Here

Also be aware of EGO. EGO is

Easing
God
Out

When we are unaware of the impact that EGO has on whatever we do, we become overburdened, because we feel that we are alone. When we keep God in the master plan, we truly understand that we were born for greatness because we were born from greatness. Pity the person who has no invisible means of support.

TIMEOUT #7

I can replant my *mental garden* with value-adding thoughts.

"To know and not do, is not yet to know"

BVAMs   Beliefs, Values, Assumptions, and
                 Memories
                         Remember . . .

1) whatever you are around you learn from,
2) what you learn you practice,
3) what you practice you become,
4) and what you become has consequences.

CODE

ENERGY

Section IV ENERGY

The Miniature Universe

*"I concentrate my energy on the challenge
of the moment, and my action helps
me to forget all else."*

AFFIRMATION

OVERVIEW

There are so many different types of energy in our miniature Universe that we take these sources for granted. Because certain types of energy sources are limited, we should be respectful and pay attention to how we use the energy sources.

Where attention goes, energy flows and results show. Very little will happen without attention. Be an attention manager. Manage your total energy field.

Energy should be expended in understanding what gives you pleasure and harmony, and determining how to achieve them. In the book entitled *Taming Your*

Gremlin by Richard D. Carson there is a discussion on
what he calls the Six Basics of Pleasure, a form of meditation. In short, he writes that basic pleasures are 1)
simply noticing, 2) choosing and playing with options,
3) staying in process, 4) remembering where you end
and all else begins—and that is your skin, 5) making
enjoying yourself a top priority, and 6) breathing properly. These six basics of pleasure are the prerequisites to
how you will assess the state of your miniature
Universe called self or the interaction between your
PEMSS (Physical, Emotional, Mental, Spiritual, Social).
For clarity, let us take a closer look at the acronym
PEMSS.

Physical: The Total Body

Emotional: One of the Self-talk affirmations of Shad
Helmstetter's which so succinctly defines
emotional is, " I am in complete control
of all the activity of my own mind—I direct its attention and I command its
thoughts—my mind accepts this direction
and it serves me well."

Mental: Your intellect, knowledge, and imagination. All of the raw material you need to
achieve.

Spiritual: A discernment. The intellect cannot do what is created for the spirit to do.

Social: We are social beings. We need each other whether we realize it or not. We are part of the energy field. When we try to be separate or isolated by ourselves, we really don't make it.

We strive to get reconnected with friends and family. Sometimes we only need a small charge. That telephone call or holiday visit may be all that is needed. Other times, it may be a need for a greater charge such as a week-long or summer visit. But we make sure that somehow we connect.

That is why we feel such a loss after someone dies. They have become separated from our energy field and we try so diligently during the mourning period to replace the pain with anything. That is why it takes a while to rebuild that power source. Sometimes we are not able to reconnect and we act and think as a burnout circuit would: no energy.

In Chapter Nine—"The Big Bang," we will examine thought as it relates to energy management. Chapter

Ten—"The Garden" and Chapter Eleven—"Learning Is Not Only Like Life, It Is Life," will address how you can cultivate your behavior to nourish and to create an amazing life. We will also discuss how learning is a continuos life process for personal growth and development.

CHAPTER NINE

"The beginning is the most important part of the work."

PLATO

THE BIG BANG

One "Big Bang" will simultaneously signal the end and the beginning of a new life: a major forest fire, a massive explosion, a jet threading itself through a needle-like tower. Just one Big Bang ends and starts life almost as quickly as the wave of a hand. What was your Big Bang? What will be your Big Bang? What will be the Big Bang that will signal you to reassess and rediscover who and where you "really" are? If you desire success or to take your life to another level, then create the harmony you deserve.

We have everything we need to recover or navigate the Big Bang. We are similar to radio stations; we are always sending and receiving information. Our eyes are like cameras and our ears are like tape recorders and every hair pore within our miniature Universe is taking in and sending out information throughout our multi-sensory being. It is not until we can comprehend the information that is traveling through and around our miniature Universe that we can be in charge of this gift. We must be able to discern between what is useful and useless. But once we have trained and raised the level of our thinking to know the difference between useful and useless, we can really be in charge of this gift we call *self*—the synchronization of the PEMSS—our miniature Universe. YES!™

We have proven to the world that we can be transformed and are capable of bouncing back from a Big Bang. Within our miniature Universe we possess all the raw materials, abilities and skills we need. Everything we need to accomplish is possible if we manage our *Thinking, Attitude, Feelings, Actions, and Results (TAFAR)*. This is our opportunity and gift to cultivate our *mental garden* which should be maintained for a harmonious, healthy, and happy life.

CHAPTER TEN

"We build our fortunes thought by thought,
For so the world was wrought.
A Thought by another name is fate,
Choose then the destiny and wait
For love brings love and hate brings hate."

VAN DYKE

THE GARDEN

We come to realize that we are not our thoughts. We are the thinker (user) of the thoughts just as we are the planter of the seeds (ideas). We have been gifted to have something to plant in our minds, the garden. Select wisely.

Do your own thinking. That does not mean that you should not listen to other people. Just do not take information at face value. Examine the information. You will reap what you sow—Garbage In, Garbage Out—Good In, Good Out. Take responsibility and make the final decision about what is to be planted in your garden. Remember,

Sow a thought, reap an action.
Sow an action, reap a habit.
Sow a habit, reap a character.
Sow a character, reap a destiny.

You have to monitor and maintain your mental garden. If you do not monitor and maintain the garden by constantly and consistently fertilizing it with positive thoughts and affirmations, the weeds in the form of doubt and CODE blockers will surface. They will creep in and begin to choke out the new growth. Weeding is difficult because the unwanted vegetation sprouts up from everywhere in various forms. Sometimes it is as aromatic as a fragrant flower and just as pretty; other times it is camouflaged to look like the good plants in your garden.

While under construction, you will receive unsolicited assistance from supporters of which some will be barriers of weed pollen. It is never your intent to be unkind to your supporters, or anyone else because a thankful heart has a continuous feast. A person who has forgotten how to be thankful has fallen asleep. What that person needs is HEART. You can extend your heartfelt gratitude in many ways. Below is an acrostic, an anchoring technique discussed in Chapter Nineteen, that may help you in communicating with your supporters and humankind.

HEART

Please . . .

Hear, and understand me.

Even if you disagree, don't make me feel wrong.

Acknowledge my great potential.

Remember my loving intention.

Tell me the truth with compassion.

Know that what you allow to enter your garden has consequences. This is why I emphasize self-talk or internal dialogue. Affirmations are a common form of self-talk and a few of mine are shared with you in Section VII. Self-talk is the only tool that I know of that will provide a continuous stream of nourishment that will turn your habits around, modify or change them, or get rid of them. Self-talk is a life-altering gift that you have been given.

CHAPTER ELEVEN

*"Great ability develops and reveals itself
increasingly with every new assignment."*

BALTASAR GRACIAN, THE ORACLE

LEARNING IS NOT ONLY LIKE LIFE, IT IS LIFE

In seeking understanding, you go from gathering and reading information to learning. As author Brian Tracy says, "Learning is not only like life, it is life." Learning is any relatively permanent change in behavior that occurs as a result of experience. You may make a paradigm shift based solely on that fact that by making the change you get what you desire.

Psychologist B. F. Skinner referred to this behavioral change as *operant conditioning*. Operant conditioning is a "behavioral theory that argues that voluntary or learned behavior is a function of its consequences." More of this theory can be studied by reading various materials by Dr. Skinner.

Fear, as discussed in Chapter Two and in Section III, can stop advancement and the learning process. Fear is neither good nor bad except thinking will make it so. *Phobophobia—The Fear of Fear* is a simplistic look at fear and tells you what you need to know to get unstuck and how to make that shift to get on with living. The book discusses how fear and discomfort will inhibit your growth and development. It also distinguishes between real fear and unwarranted fear. Unwarranted fear is learned or conditioned fear, and many do not realize that it can be changed. It is a matter of developing some strategies, gain knowledge of the subject matter, and seek understanding to eliminate the unwarranted fear from your life. Again, this is determining what is useful and what is useless. Doing away with the unwarranted fear is like getting rid of a logjam which is another CODE blocker. Once you remove the logjam, you begin to think freely and you are back on track again.

A brief example of this is the person who has a snake phobia. He sees little vines on the side of a road and his immediate reaction is to jump or run away screaming. The vines looked like snakes and the person believed them to be snakes. Further inspection demonstrates that the perceived snakes are vines. Look at the energy wasted on an unwarranted fear. Just thinking the thought was enough to trigger a dysfunctional response. A desired behavior can be created by transforming your thought patterns.

We all have unsolicited supporters who share powerful nourishing information to add to our mental gardens. Some of the authors are unknown to me, however, I would like to share this awesome poem that summarizes some of my concepts.

"LEARNING IS NOT ONLY LIKE LIFE, IT IS LIFE"

We are the sum total of what we have been told and taught, and sold and bought.
No one knows enough to be a pessimist.
Learning is the gold that I place in the bank of my own mind,
and I invest in my mind every day.
Avoid saying, I already know that.
When all else fails, there is always hope.
Your imagination must not be a storehouse for your fears.
Where attention goes, energy flows and results show.
The greatest barrier to self-fulfillment is fear combined with ignorance.

YIKES! Snakes!

This exemplifies a perceived fear or an unwarranted fear and a
tremendous amount of expended energy.

I can't believe my eyes! These snakes are just vines.

The Reality Check

Oscar and Hallie

"ONE MOMENT IN A LIFE'S STORY"

"The Big O" Oscar Robertson

"When I grew up in Indy on Colton St., I did not realize what needs the families had or ever hoped to have. There wasn't any money and the boys on the street played sports and told you things about life. No money, no place to go, and very little to do—What's left?—sports—BASKETBALL!

I first met Hallie Bryant through my older brother Bailey on the Lockefield playground called The Dustbowl. Hallie was a masterful player who was always under control, and the other players respected that about him. Watching the Crispus Attucks High School team play and win their first state tournament really inspired me. Hallie, at guard, became a hero for me to emulate and match his accomplishments. I would sit and watch his movements, footwork, mannerisms, and grace. I wanted to be that player, Hallie Bryant.

ONE MOMENT . . . (Continued)

Breaking the CODE reminded me of my early days in Charlotte, Tennessee and how young minds occupy their time playing in the woods or just sitting on a fence post and counting cars that go by. The small simple things in life sometimes make you the happiest. People should read this book to investigate their inner feelings and thought processes to let them feel good about communicating with others and try to determine the importance of why they are here. I am very pleased that I know Hallie Bryant for he has been a guiding light for me.

"The Big O"

INTERMISSION

THE HALF-TIME SHOW

Featuring

A Sneak Preview of Some of Hallie's Scrapbook Moments

HALLIE BRYANT -- WITH NEW GLOBETROTTER OWNERS (l-r) POTTER PALMER, JOHN O'NEIL AND GEORGE GILLETT -- BECOMES FIRST PLAYER TO MOVE INTO THE ORGANIZATION'S ADVANCE PUBLICITY DEPARTMENT.

"Hallie Bryant Becomes the First Player to Move into the Globetrotter Organization's Advance Publicity Department"

Deloris and Hallie with friends, as Hallie was inducted into the Indiana University Athletic Hall of fame. Pictured (L to R) Deloris Hayes, Hallie Bryant, Judy Doninger, Ann Carpenter, and Clarence Doninger, former Director of Athletics for Indiana University.

Indiana High School Athletic Association (IHSAA) Hall of Fame Banquet. Pictured with Hallie are former Globetrotters: Bailey "Flap" Robertson, "Wee" Willie Gardner, Hallie Bryant, and "The Big O" Oscar Robertson.

Hallie pictured with Bob Collins, sports columnist for the The Indianapolis Star. (L to R) Hallie, Bob Collins, (center) Bailey "Flap" Robertson, (back row) Cleveland Harp, and "Wee" Willie Gardner.

Pictured with
Hallie Bryant in
Southern Rhodesia
are Globetrotter
Teammates JC Gipson and
Bob "Showboat" Hall.

Salisbury, Southern Rhodesia

Globetrotter teammate, Tony
Wilcox (left) and Hallie Bryant
had the opportunity to receive
some pointers on their jump-
shots from a local horse jockey
at the racetrack.

Phoenix, AZ. Hallie enjoying a playful moment during a PR promotion break for the Globetrotters is pictured with his lifelong friend Bill Shover.

The Great Satchel Paige and Hallie discuss Paige's philosophy on the now famous phrase "don't look back—something might be gaining on you."

Pictured with Hallie is Herman B. Wells, a former chancellor of Indiana University, who was instrumental in breaking the racial barrier for Big 10 Conference basketball.

Marques Haynes, the great basketball dribbling magician, is pictured with Hallie Bryant before a basketball clinic in Honolulu, Hawaii.

Hallie and Marques

Fred "Curly" Neal, the great basketball dribbling magician, is pictured with Hallie Bryant before a basketball clinic at the Chicago Stadium.

"Curly" and Hallie

Hallie Bryant is presented a prestigious award from the then mayor of Indianapolis, Richard Lugar, current United States Senator.

Philadelphia 76er

Wilt "The Stilt" Chamberlain takes a moment to pose with his friend, Hallie, after a game.

Australia

The Globetrotters are pictured with the 1964 "Miss Adelaide." First row (L to R) Hallie Bryant, Jackie Jackson, Miss Adelaide, David Gaines, and Curly Neal. Top row Bobby Milton, Tony Wilcox, JC Gipson, John Gibson, and Norman JR Lee.

REUNION TIME

Friends gather to support Hallie and Deloris as Hallie gets inducted into the Indiana University Athletic Hall of Fame. Pictured left to right are Dr. Greg Bell, Hallie, Deloris, Celine and Wally Choice. (Back Row) Mary Bell, "Sweet" Charlie Brown, Wilma Smith, Yvonne and Lenny Robinson, George Taliafero, and Bill Garrett Jr.

Can you find Regis Philbin and Joey Bishop?

Hallie Bryant and the Globetrotters featured on the Joey Bishop Show in the early sixties. If you guessed that Joey Bishop is the one with the ball, you are correct. Regis Philbin, the host of the popular TV game show "Who Wants To Be A Millionaire?" is the man with the shorts on facing Joey Bishop.

HARLEM GLOBETROTTERS OF 1960–61 -- Top row, left to right: W.S. Welch, unit manager; Tony Wilcox, J.C. Gipson, Ben Jackson, Willis Thomas, Bob (Showboat) Hall. Bottom, left to right: Ermer Robinson, Hallie Bryant, Bobby Milton, Joe Bourne, Owner-Coach Abe Saperstein.

The Man with the Vision

Featured with the Harlem Globetrotters of 1960–61 is the Owner-Coach Abe Saperstein.

Hallie pictured with the late Tom Binford, former track chief steward for the 500 mile Indianapolis Motor Speedway (Indy 500).

Pictured left to right are Hallie, Deloris Hayes, Tom Binford, and his wife, Kai Binford.

HALLIE BRYANT   *Former Globetrotter*

In the Moment

Hallie "The Comet" Bryant

"NO PIE IN THE FACE PLEASE!"

After a taped session for the television program, the Wide World of Sports, comedian, Soupy Sales, joined us to go over some game plays.

Ed McMahon takes a break with Globetrotters (l to r) David Latin, Jimmy Blacklock, Charles "Tex" Harrison, an onlooker, Bobby Milton (with the ball), and Hallie Bryant after a major grand opening in Texas.

"Tom, Dick, and Hallie"

This is not *just* your usual "Tom, Dick, and Hallie". Pictured with Hallie are the NBA stars Tom and Dick Van Arsdale, the only twins inducted in to the Indiana High School Athletic Association (IHSAA) as co- Mr. Basketball.

Indiana University's Hurrying Hoosiers

Hallie "The Comet" Bryant

"For Now—That's All Folks"

The International Logo
for
"The Comet"

Section V HALLIE'S HABITS FOR PERSONAL SUCCESS

The Rules of the Game Called "Life"

> *"Become aware of your habits.*
> *Your mind is like a garden,*
> *and it can be cultivated*
> *or allowed to run wild."*

> JAMES ALLEN, AUTHOR OF *As A Man Thinketh*

OVERVIEW

Many authors have stated and I wholeheartedly agree that good habits are hard to form but easy to live with. Bad habits are easy to form but hard to live with. We use a great deal of our energy in a nonproductive way, sometimes without even knowing it. For instance, we use energy robbing language like SICO—*Should've, If only, Could've, and Oh, my God.* We need to abandon SICO because it is one of the insidious habits of wasting time.

Another habit of wasting energy is to be overly anxious or frightened. For example, the report is late. What will the instructor say? How will the boss react? I stayed out later than anticipated. Will I be in the doghouse for

the next week? These actions will definitely have consequences. Rarely are you the one to determine the consequences, so why are you expending so much energy
worrying about the outcome?

A great use of energy would have been to deal with
each issue up-front. Why is the report late? If you
needed more time it could have been effectively com-
municated. If what you are doing does not hurt you,
your spouse, or anyone else, why not call and state that
you will be late? Oh, it will cause an argument? It does
not sound as if you are living a harmonious life. This is
the point. Some energy will escape and we cannot prevent that action. But what we can prevent is the waste
of energy in the form of punishment, heartache, or
costly divorce settlements.

That energy running rampant is the essence of you.
When we have a mental breakdown or some act that
renders us to believing that we are the victim, it is because we are probably not using our imagination in a
useful way. If we do not know how to use our imagination properly, it will mess up our life. By managing your
thinking, you manage your life. Thinking should be
taught in school as Thinking 101 and Thinking 102.
Remember, good habits are hard to form but easy to
live with. Bad habits are easy to form but hard to live
with—again cause and effect.

I know that you can get side-tracked from your tasks causing you to develop some undesirable habits, but it is crucial that you remain focused on issues before they become distractions. We look at some of Hallie's habits in the next chapter and take a closer look at how to examine habits in Chapter Thirteen.

CHAPTER TWELVE

"He is able who thinks he is able."

BUDDHA

HALLIE'S HABITS

1. Begin the day with meditation. (Plant what is useful for you. Of all the things that I have to be grateful for, I am grateful to see another day.)

2. Breathe and renew the inner spirit. (Breathe deeply by inhaling through your nose and slowly exhaling through your mouth.)

3. Walk to exercise and to get focused on the day. (Discover how wonderful it is to remove yourself from life's distractions. By doing so, you are able to Review, Register, Recall, and Retain *The 4Rs*)

4. Talk to yourself and recite your affirmations. (Say YES!™ from the abdomen like you believe it.)

5. Slip into the GAP and remember to Relax, Breathe and Move Gracefully (RBMG) several times a day.

6. Manage your Beliefs, Values, Assumptions, and Memories BVAMs.

7. End the day with meditation by giving thanks to the Creator.

CHAPTER THIRTEEN

*"(A) Habit is . . . not to be flung out of
the window by any man, but
coaxed downstairs a step at a time."*

MARK TWAIN

EXAMINE THE HABIT

Habits, whether useful or useless, are conditioned reactions; responding without consciously thinking. First, you want to identify the habit. Of course there will be more than one, but we will take them one at a time. Remember, "inch by inch it's a cinch, by the yard it's hard. The next action you want to take is to examine the habit." My father used to tell me, "If you just know the *how* son, you only have the half of it. You need to know the *why*." I interpret this as the cause and affect. Finally, ask yourself two questions, 1) what is it in your belief system that causes this unacceptable behavior, and 2) why do I choose to act this way?

If one is being synthetic and knows it, one should

make the change to be authentic and reap the reward. I used to question people's motives when they knew better and still behaved in the same negative manner. I have come to know that a person will only do better when their awareness expands.

It is important to examine our habits because we want to be OK with ourselves. Our "OK-ness" is an indication of how we view the world and others. It is our mental framework that dictates our reality. We see the world based on how we are and not the way it is. Perception is a mirror—a reflection of our self-image and behavior. We cannot perform above the level of our self-image.

Behavior is learned and whatever is learned can be modified or unlearned. There is nothing to be afraid of. As you look into your garden and do not like what you see, cultivate it by pulling up the weeds or by replacing old, outdated information or misinformation with new positive thoughts. Separate your behavior from your essence because you are not your behavior. You are not your behavior, but you are responsible for it.

CHAPTER FOURTEEN

"Be impeccable with your word."

DON MIGUEL RUIZ

MANAGE YOUR WORDS—(Idealize It, Verbalize It, VIsualize It, Emotionalize It, and Realize It)

Brian Tracy is one of the foremost authorities on human behavior. In studying the principles above, I have created the Hallieism called IVVER. I apply this Hallieism with regard to how I anchor my words and concepts. This is my abbreviated version and adaptation for these terms.

Idealize It: Imagine things not as they are at the moment, but as you would have them to be.

Verbalize It: Vocalize it. Say it out loud with convictions—at least three times.

Visualize It: See it clearly, vividly, intensely.

Emotionalize It: Allow your controlled feelings to flow and remain in charge of them.

Realize It: Bring it to life. Be able to touch it. Claim it!

If we allow ourselves to become conscious of what we say, and how we express what we say, we will gain tremendous power. We need to be impeccable with our words. Language spoken in terms of "The 3Cs", *complaining, condemning,* and *criticizing,* are poison to the thinking process. They will rob us of our energy, make us dysfunctional, and will keep us steeped in fear. Language inside of us can tie us up into knots. Blaming others or ourselves is self-defeating. There is no gain— in blame—only pain. Blaming imprisons us and becomes injurious to our total health. It can become so much of an addiction or habit that we are not aware that we are even doing it. Someone can tell us that we are doing something and we'll say, "No way!"

It is said that there is nothing more powerful than the spoken word. My guess is that words can evoke a plethora of emotions. My definition of civilization is *well-managed emotions.* Author Jim Rohn, discusses well-managed emotions in his book titled, *Take Charge of Your Life.* Having well-managed emotions has been the "Power of The Comet". With all of the losses, disappointments, and challenges that I endured not only in sports, but in life, God and my support system enabled me to overcome the undesirable circumstances and manage my emotions. That which will not kill you will make you stronger. As Brian Tracy said that every situation is a positive situation if viewed as an opportunity for growth and self-mastery, I agree. **YES!**™

Regardless of the undesirable circumstances, I have never lost my ability to be empathetic. Empathy is the willingness and the ability to see another person through that person's eyes. I have spoken to many business leaders and sales forces and I share with them the following:

EMPATHY

If you can see Sam Jones through Sam Jones' eyes,

you can sell Sam Jones what Sam Jones buys.

Well-managed words, to yourself and others, will positively impact your life. You move from knowledge to understanding. Remember, knowledge is just answers to questions. Knowledge alone is not enough. Wisdom is knowing what to do with that knowledge. Do not forget to make it PUUR. Make it Purposeful, Useful, Understandable, and Relevant.

CHAPTER FIFTEEN

"If we don't change, we don't grow.
If we don't grow, we aren't really living . . .
Changes are not only possible and predictable,
but to deny them is to be an accomplice
to one's own vegetation."

GAIL SHEEHY
Author of *Pathfinders:*
Predictable Crises of Adult Life

FEAR NO MORE—CHANGE IS ABOUT EXECUTION, REPETITION, SUCCESSES, CONFIDENCE, HABIT, AND BELIEF

In the year of 1900 William James said that the greatest discovery of our time was not the automobile or the electric light bulb, but the fact that man *can* change by changing his inner attitude of mind. As discussed in Chapter Four, people thought that they had no control, or very little control, over themselves. They discovered that they did not have to be locked into their habits. They felt relieved that they did not have to be like their disappointing uncle or disillusioned aunt or some other unsuccessful relative.

By showing people how to be aware of their habits,

how to identify them, and most importantly, how to erase and replace them will make it a freeing experience. This whole process will allow people to achieve or maintain inner harmony.

People fear change. The reason for this reaction is that people fear the uncertainty of change and believe that they would be worse off if they changed. The simplest formula to preparing yourself for change is to be well-rested with an open-mind. You want to set the stage for the growth process. Being well-rested will help you to think clearly.

Habits are honed by fear. There is healthy fear and there is unhealthy fear. Step outside of the situation to determine which fear is useful and which is useless. Once you are able to make that distinction, you will be able to remove the negative or unwarranted fear and process the healthy fear. Keep in mind that *fear* is energy running rampant. Referring back to our example in Chapter 11, where the rope appeared to be a snake, once you see that it is a rope and not a snake, you should say "Thank you, fearful habit, for revealing yourself to me so that I can consciously know what to do."

To establish a fearless approach to change, let us look at the following model Exhibit 4, the ERSCHB tool as mentioned in Chapter Four.

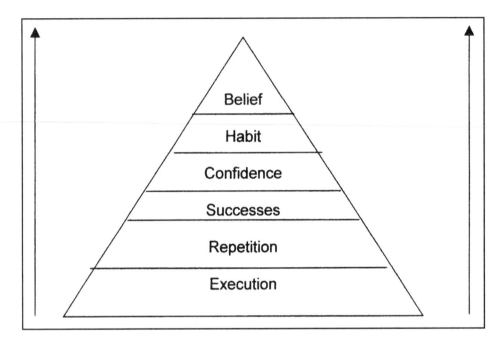

Exhibit 4. One of the greatest tools to help us effectuate change by changing a habit is the ERSCHB tool (*Execution, Repetition, Successes, Confidence, Habit, and Belief Tool*). This system refers to the programming in place and the reprogramming to effectuate the change.

1. **Execution** is actually getting started to examine or assess the present situation. Take action now. Learn how to self-correct with tenderness.

2. **Repetition** is the Mother of Successes and how we learn. Repetition erases the old habit while simultaneously replacing the old habit with the new one. Law of substitution. Repetition is the anchor. Walk your talk. Examine often and self-correct.

3. **Successes** build confidence and self-esteem. A discussion of the Four Stages of Learning in Chapter Sixteen will further clarify successes. Start out small. The more successes you have, the more you believe in yourself. Enough successes will build your confidence and self-esteem to a level that you begin to believe that you can CBA—Conceive It, Believe It, and Achieve It.

4. **Confidence** is a positive inner strength but not arrogance. Increased confidence allows for the continuation of the process.

5. **Habits** are what you establish when you are in the flow. You do it without thinking, and unconscious behavior.

6. **Belief** is beyond the intellect. It is the knowing and is deeply-rooted in our mind.

As in anything we do, we should ask the **WIIFM** question, "What's In It For Me?" When we can see the "Big Picture" we are motivated to continue our process and the following is how I invite you to see the "Big Picture"—**The Mastery of the Art of Living**.

A MASTER IN THE ART OF LIVING

A master in the art of living
draws no sharp distinction between
his work and his play,
his labor and his leisure,
his mind and his body,
his education and his recreation.
He hardly knows which is which.
He simply pursues his vision of excellence through
    whatever
he is doing and leaves others to determine whether
he is working or playing.
To himself, he always seems to be doing both.

Author Unknown

Section VI   TOOLS FOR LEARNING

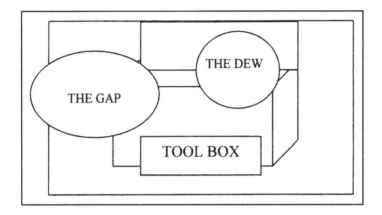

OVERVIEW

The GAP, which is also known as "The Pause," is the time that you allow God or the power that you honor greater than yourself to speak to you. The GAP is the silence. Be still and you will come to know. We need that silence to help us to relax, rejuvenate, re-focus, and reach all that we desire.

Anytime that you have debilitating thoughts, feel powerless or lost, slip into the GAP. It is the only place that you will find divineness. When we encounter conflicts or stress, we should, as stated by Dr. DeePak Chopra, a renowned Eastern philosopher, 1) slip into the GAP, 2) have the desire, 3) release the attachment to the outcome, and 3) let the Universe take care of the details. It will anyway.

When I think about my past, I recall that I was too naïve to hate. If I had been vindictive as I have witnessed others being, I might have been killed because of the contagious diseases CODE blockers of hatred, envy, jealousy, and pettiness can cause. Again, because of God and my support system I usually was able to manifest the notion of ease instead of disease. I chose to slip into the GAP and allowed my true self or the "Big Me" to guide me. That way it was possible for divine thoughts to be manifested in the silence. Remember the free flowing mode will always give you answers. Avoid the CODE blockers. As a wise man once said, "get your bloated nothingness out of the paths of your divine circuits!" YES!™

Many successful athletes, as well as other business people, clergymen, and presenters have a ritual before entering their event. My ritual was a mental process where I would slip into the GAP. When I was playing basketball, I would remind myself that I had practiced and that I was prepared for whatever might happen on the court. For the most part, in retrospect, I played at a level of unconscious competence. All I needed was to have faith and the DEW—Desire, Energy, and Willingness.

Chapter Sixteen

"It is not enough to make(force) someone to learn,
you must make them want to learn!"

Unknown

FOUR STAGES OF LEARNING

When we look at Dr. Abraham Maslow's *Four Stages of Learning* we are talking about the following:

Unconscious Incompetence—In this stage you have little experience or skill in trying to accomplish a certain task or effort. *You do not know that you do not know.*

Conscious Incompetence—As your awareness evolves into this stage, you begin to realize how little you know. It is the stage where you know you can't do something, and you don't know how to take care of it. *You know that you do not know.*

Conscious Competence—This stage creates a field of positive energy all around you. Self-esteem is high because you are pleased with yourself in knowing that you know what you are doing and that you realize how much you have learned. *You know what you know.*

Unconscious Competence—This is the place of almost perfect harmony. A place where there is little or no difference between what the physical body has practiced to perfection and the emotional, spiritual, and social mind has learned. This is where you can do something freely and without thinking about it. *You know what you know and you perform without thinking about it.*

In the *Unconscious Incompetent* stage it is virtually impossible to negatively impact your self-esteem because you are totally unaware of what you do not know. It is said that, "you are at the *false confidence* phase that coexists with ignorance." Self-esteem is not impacted until the second stage of learning.

Some consider the *Conscious Incompetence* stage to be a painful stage because of the stress many place on themselves for not knowing or possessing the skills they need to move forward. I consider this the enlightened stage and an opportunity to grow. All is not lost in this stage because learning begins with acknowledging what you don't know which we refer to as awareness, and success begins with the desire, and willingness to expend the energy to learn.

At this stage in the learning cycle, a person is enabled to *build* on his strengths, *overcome* his weaknesses, and *tolerate* his limitations (BOT-Build, Overcome, Tolerate). Please understand that much learning occurs at this stage. As one anchors his thoughts, improves his skills, and manages his thoughts, emotions, and actions, his body will be in harmony or in balance with his mind and he will begin to evolve into stage three, conscious competence.

In the *Conscious Competence* stage you spend much of your time thinking about what is happening and what is going to be next. Dr. Abraham Maslow's studies found that "most people spend considerably more time here than in the first two stages. It is also a plateau where many choose to remain. However, true self-mastery is not attained until the fourth stage of learning."

Unconscious Competence stage of learning is natural and second nature to you. You are free to enjoy whatever endeavor, wherever you are, at the moment. It is like learning how to ride a bicycle or learning to walk. After you have learned how to do these activities you just do it. This stage is represented by the following masters of their professions: Larry Bird, Magic Johnson, Michael Jordan, Oscar Robertson, and Isiah Thomas on the basketball court; Tiger Woods on the golf course, Greg Louganis on the diving board, Joe Montana on the football field; Ted Williams, Babe Ruth, and Hank Aaron on the baseball field, Venus and Serena Williams on the tennis court. Other great masters of their professions are Jack Welch and Lee Iacocca leading major corporations, Dr. Martin Luther King delivering an address, and Oprah Winfrey as a talk show host. Self-mastery is what all of the aforementioned individuals have achieved along with presenters like Steven Covey speaking on the *Seven Habits of Highly Effective People*, or me delivering a keynote address to 10,000 attendees or going down the court executing a game-winning shot.

If you are fortunate enough to be backstage before a major event or close enough to the field, court, or arena when an athlete is readying himself or herself for the event, you will almost always see them take a *deep* breath. That is when they allow themselves to slip into the **GAP** for that moment of silence to bring to their minds all of the things they need to manage their thoughts, emotions, and actions. All of this is accomplished by simply remembering to RBMG—relax, breathe, and move gracefully. The people who are at stage four of the learning stages are not worried about the outcomes, because of muscle memory. Their minds are free to perform without fear of failure because they have trained their muscles to respond automatically. This level of self-mastery belongs to the true professionals of their trade.

I include a fifth stage when I make my presentations. The fifth stage is the bonus. When you teach, you are learning and you become what you teach. You teach yourself first. Then you teach someone else and it comes back to you.

A LESSON IN LEARNING

We Learn What We Teach

We Teach What We Learn,

and

We Become What We Teach.

Or, simply put,

Learn It → Teach It → Own It

Chapter Seventeen

"Vision is the art of seeing the invisible."

AUTHOR UNKNOWN

YOU NEED THE FBI

Call in the FBI to solve problems or to relieve stress. When problems or stress mount up, remember to first RBMG. Relax, breathe, and move gracefully. Then pursue understanding and clarity. Take yourself through a visualization and call on the FBI—Faith, Belief, and Imagination. Have faith that all will be fine in the fullness of time. Belief is the law of life and imagination is the place where things are created.

Solving problems and releasing stress is a process and an inside job. At times some things can be overwhelming. In the words of Dr. Maxwell Maltz, when unfavorable things come across our mind CRAFT it. Cancel it, Replace it, Affirm it, Focus it, and Train it. YES!™

Dig deep into your imagination, stir it up. Pull from your well-cultivated mental garden of ideas, solutions, and affirmations. Create a mental piggybank. You need to pre-load or deposit into the piggybank your harvested ideas, solutions, and affirmations. Then when they are needed you can make quick withdrawals. Remember that repetition is the mother of successes and by reciting your affirmations on a regular basis, once daily at a minimum, your bank will be rich in all you need to survive.

Positive **T**houghts and **A**ffirmations

Deposit your "Positive Thoughts and Affirmations" in your mental garden which is also known as your private piggy bank! We can always use our PTAs to get us through difficult times and in overcoming challenges. If you do not monitor and maintain the garden by constantly and consistently fertilizing it with positive thoughts and affirmations, the weeds in the form of doubt and CODE blockers will surface.

Section VII   MAKING IT STICK AND AFFIRMATIONS

OVERVIEW

The bonding glue of all glues is the word **YES!**™ Yes seals it. This affirmation must come from within. Not from the surface you—not from a shallow place—but from the depths of your soul. The power of this small three-letter word can not be overstated. It is the glue that binds you to your thoughts words, and actions.

> **YOUR**
> **ENERGY**
> **SOURCE**™

The power in hearing people say **YES!**™ as I teach this technique to people across the country is inspiring. As a certified self-talk trainer, I have had many opportunities to test and confirm this **YES!**™ concept with the participants as well as the other principles in this book. These principles have worked for others and they will work for you.

AFFIRMATIONS

A#1

There is another way of looking at the world and I am determined to find it.

(This allows me to make a paradigm shift such as thinking outside of the box. I can clear the slate and view things from different perspectives.)

A #2

I am not the thought I am the thinker of the thoughts. I therefore can control my attitude about life.

A #3

We do not see with the eyes, we see through the eyes.

(Our mental framework dictates our reality. If you do not like your present situation, re-frame it. Use the ER-SCHB Tool. It works like magic!)

A #4

I choose to live in the present. I believe in the law of substitution. I will erase those things that cause me stress and replace with positive thoughts and energy.

I will learn from the past, plan for the future, and live in the now.

(LPL)

A #5

When I am troubled I will Let go, Lighten up, and Let God.

A #6

Today, I choose to see myself as having an unlimited capacity for creativity, problem solving and growth.

A #7

Never believe that the limits of my present view are the limits of my possibilities.

A #8

I seek love. Love is harmony. I am created for harmony **YES!**™

A #9

Let me recognize today that the bottom line of all my problems, regardless of their form, is the fear of separation.

A #10

I choose peace and live by the MUFIT principle—Mercy, Understanding, Forgiveness, Imagination, and Truth.

MUFIT Mercy is a form of useful empathy. Understanding forgiveness of self first which is one of the toughest things to do. Imagination is imagineering and tweaking the thoughts being recreated—re-framing. Truth is reality and it will not go away. It is not always the way we want it but the way it is. It is the only thing that will set you free.

A #11

Forgiveness will release me today from all personal suffering and feeling of loss.

A #12

I am free to make choices. The Creator of Everything has already designed me for success. All things are possible when using the FBI.(Faith, Belief, and Imagination)

A #13

I know to SPR. When I am confronted with a *Stimulus*, I will *Pause*, and then *Respond*.

A #14

I will periodically slip into the GAP during the day to refresh my spirit.

CHAPTER EIGHTEEN

"You gain strength, courage, and confidence by every experience in which you really stop to look fear in the face."

ELEANOR ROOSEVELT

R2A2—"RECOGNIZE, RELATE—ASSIMILATE, APPLY"

W. CLEMENT STONE

Before any application of information can occur, especially the application of new information or thoughts, it is essential to first recognize what you have learned. Recognize and determine the importance and value of the new thoughts and processes. Get a clear vision of and validate how what you knew and what you have learned impact your thinking process. You need to be able to relate to the new information in such a way that when you process the information, you too can explain it, teach it, expand it, and own it. By relating or recounting the information and making it personal, it will trigger the natural process of internalizing the information and making it real to you. Once you are able to make it real, the process will evolve to assimilation.

To assimilate is to absorb and internalize the information and make it yours. The new thoughts become relevant and a part of your belief system. It develops as a part of your essence. You elevate to the Unconscious Competent level of learning. When you assimilate new thoughts you are able to manage your emotions, words, and actions effortlessly.

The application of "how you manage yourself" and "why you manage yourself" a certain way, becomes apparent in the application process of the formula. To develop a seamless transition of applying the new and/or enhanced information you have learned, continue on to Chapter Nineteen and learn how to develop ways to anchor the thoughts through memory techniques and self-talk.

CHAPTER NINETEEN

"Warning, my thoughts may turn to words at any moment."

UNKNOWN

"Capture your thoughts and anchor them."

O'MERRIAL BUTCHEE

THE QUADRANGLE FORMULA TO ANCHORING THE THOUGHTS: MNEMONICS, ACROSTICS, SELF-TALK, AND OTHER TOOLS

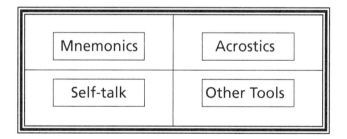

ANCHOR THE THOUGHTS

Embrace the idea of learning. Throughout life, oftentimes we were taught the "how," but the "why" was omitted. That is incomplete learning. In some cases perhaps you were too young to remember "big words" like mnemonics but I do recall learning onomatopoeia at a very early age. By the way, that *onomatopoeia* means the formation of a word associated with its sound such as sizzle—the sound bacon makes when frying in a pan. There are several forms or creative ways to remember terms and concepts. The conscious choice we use to anchor information may be based primarily on our learning style. Briefly, there are three dominant learning styles: audio, visual, and kinesthetic. The audio style refers to the person who likes to listen to information being delivered to him or her based on sermons or lectures. The visual person wants to see the subject matter. Draw that person a mental or physical picture. Use graphics. The kinesthetic learner enjoys hands-on action and physical movement. Tell a kinesthetic person to "hold on to" a dream or "to grasp" an idea.

Remembering concepts or anchoring thoughts is similar to what you do when learning how to ride a bicycle. At first, to gain comfort, training wheels are placed on the bicycle to help you steady yourself. As you grow and mature in knowledge and get a feel for proper balance, the wheels come off and you are on your way.

We help our brain remember changes, new techniques, terminology, etc. in a similar manner. We put on "Braining Wheels (mental training wheels for the brain like the training wheels for the bicycle) to help us to remember and/or to anchor thoughts and concepts. Those Braining Wheels are known as acronyms, mnemonics, similes, metaphors, pictures, self-talk and any other tools that help us achieve our goal. Some individuals relate information to songs in order to anchor their materials. We use whatever techniques that are more agreeable to our learning style whether the style is audio, visual, or kinesthetic.

We have chosen to discuss the more involved memory techniques or mental training wheels such as *mnemonics, acrostics*, and a powerful tool that I use everyday called *self-talk*. As you continue to grow and manage yourself by managing your thoughts, words, and actions, you can use these techniques to assist you to retain the new information and/or insights. If you recall, we said that knowledge is one level of the process, but it is the continuous repetition of that knowledge that strengthens beliefs, and change the old habits which allows for the new habits and beliefs to "stick."

MNEMONICS

Mnemonics is a memory technique that will allow you to recall difficult information. The basic principle of mnemonics is to use as many functions of the human brain (engaging the left and the right sides of the brain) to code information. This is not a new technique. Many mnemonics we learned in early learning and discarded them as if they were irrelevant in more advance learning situations. Many successful people, especially doctors, who must learn many terms as it relates to the body, uses memory techniques as described here to learn new terminology. Some familiar mnemonics are illustrated on the next page.

Now you have the name to associate with the technique. The good news is that there are no principles or laws that will prohibit you from creating anchoring tools to assist you in your learning process. Do not forget to practice this technique as well as other techniques. Repetition reinforces belief, learning, and understanding. Please remember, that in anything that you pursue, make sure that you know your purpose and get the correct understanding. **YES!**™

ACROSTICS

What are acrostics? You are already somewhat familiar with them. I have used them throughout this book to help you anchor your thoughts. I have shared some of my acrostics with you to help you remember certain

MNEMONICS

All Cows Eat Grass → A C E G

>Musically speaking, the above letters are the notes represented on the bass clef of the musical scale from the bottom to the top.

Every Good Boy Does Fine → E G B D F

>The notes represented by the lines on the treble clef from the bottom to the top

30 days hath September
April, June and November
All the rest have 31 except for
February which has 28

This rhyme helps you to remember what months have 30 days in them.

concepts such as in the poem illustrated in Chapter Ten called HEART. I use a slight variation of acrostic-like acronyms when we discussed PEMSS and BVAMS. One of my favorite acrostics is the expression below:

If you examine the first letters of each word the letters form the word FAITH. That is what faith means to me. Father and I together here on Earth. The acrostic-

FAITH:

Father

And

I

Together

Here

like acronym is often used when I make up a word that I can identify with such as PEMSS pronounced "pems" which sounds like "gems" which is enough to anchor the following concept:

PEMSS

Physical

Emotional

Mental

Spiritual

Social

Of course, it is one thing for me to show and explain to you the concept of acrostics but it is up to you to develop personal acrostics to assist you in anchoring new thoughts. Remember if it is your work it is your reward.

Following is a list of several of my favorite acrostics.

How	Success	Concise
Optimistic	Personality	Opportunity
People	Integrity	Measurable
Exist	Responsibility	Meaningful
	Intelligence	Investment
	Time	Time

These acrostics assist me in remembering the basics of three seminars on HOPE, SPIRIT, and the power to COMMIT in goal setting.

SELF-TALK

Self-talk is a powerful tool to constantly feed your subconscious mind the positive information that will allow you to believe you can achieve almost anything you desire. The will to do springs from the knowledge that we can do. Researchers have said that 95% of our feelings come from our inner dialogue. The inner dialogue will dictate how we view the world.

We are always creating in our minds with our self-talk. The language of the mind is images and pictures. The mind readily processes these images consciously or unconsciously, whether they are positive or negative. Our explanatory self is our inner dialogue that is always explaining things to .us. When we ask ourselves questions, how we answer them and what our responses are really determines our self-image. We are asking and answering questions all day long. It is impossible to end the dialogue with ourselves, even when we are sleeping. We have a concert going on all of the time that will dictate our self-image. We cannot rise above our self-image. Our self-image or self-identity is a reflection of our mental framework. This reflection represents our thought patterns which dictates our reality. Perception is a mirror not a fact. Truth is a perception: yours or mine. Reality is what is. What makes something true to you comes from your beliefs, values, assumptions, and memories. Remember, the one conversation you cannot escape is the one you have with yourself. Once you can manage your self-talk, you can manage your life.

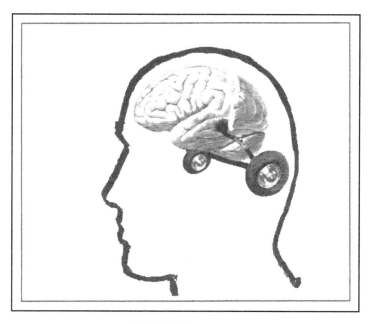

BRAINING WHEELS

Whenever we undertake a new task these "Braining Wheels" or reinforcing mental training wheels can be very helpful: particularly, when trying to change a habit, anchor new thoughts, or concepts.

Section VIII POST-GAME INTERVIEW

"We make a living by what we get,
we make a life by what we give."

AUTHOR UNKNOWN

THE CONCLUSION

As I sit here with O'Merrial and as we review the instant replays of our conversations over the past year, I realize that sometimes all you need is somebody to believe in you. We all need a strong support system to guide us and to be there for us even when we doubt ourselves.

I did not break the **CODE** by myself. No man or woman is an island. I had God, and with the assistance of my family, friends, and my dog, *I Know,* I was able to decipher the CODE. This allowed me to write it as I saw it and pass the information on to you. I consolidated this information from my personal WOW (Well of Wisdom). I used what I needed and threw the rest back for another time or for someone else to take a sip. It will be there when it is needed and I can never give more than I will receive from my *Well*!

Imagine for a moment how wonderful life would be if all the forces *Appetite, Passion, Prejudice, Greed, Love, Fear, Environment,* and *Habit* are balanced with Richard Carlson's *Six Basics of Pleasure:* simply noticing, choosing and playing with options, staying in process, remembering where you end and all else begins—and that's your skin, making enjoying yourself a top priority, and breathing properly.

Harmony manifests itself in all you say and do. Life then becomes all those things that are possible and more exciting than ever imagined.

Our final thought is that you have choices. If you like the way your life is, we have given you the tools in this book to maintain that mental garden and we have given you what you need to nourish it and keep it free from weeds or code blockers. If you do not like what your present circumstances are or the present state of the mental garden (the mind) that you have created, remember, that you can self-correct or reprogram your current thought processes by mentally erasing and replacing unwanted thoughts or habits.

I watch these principles unfold in much of the work my friends and colleagues participate in on a daily basis.

Wally Choice was the second African-American basket-ball player at Indiana University. He and his wife, Celine, who are founders of the program called "Grass Roots" in Montclair, New Jersey, exhibit many of the principles

Wally Choice, Hallie Bryant and
the 1956 Decathlon Champion, Milt Campbell

Photograph L

discussed in this book. For many years they have done an outstanding job in preparing our youth for the future. Photograph L is a picture of Hallie, Milt Campbell and Wally taken after a youth program. The Montclair Grass Roots Program helps young boys and girls to develop themselves by letting them know that they too have choices and that the organization believes in them. True success is demonstrated when you give back.

We all need someone to believe in, as we need someone to believe in us. When things get tough, and they will, know that you are not alone and that I believe in you. I will leave you with a great inspirational poem by my dear friend, Dr. Greg Bell, entitled *I Believe In You*.

Dr. Gregory Bell, Author of "I Believe in You"

Photograph M

I BELIEVE IN YOU

There seems to be no limit as to what a man can do
If he's buoyed up by the current of an "I believe in you."
He can climb the highest mountain, swim the widest sea,
He can be whatever person he believes himself to be.

Now, when I say a man can do these things, I hope you
know
That a woman, too, can match a man and go where he can
go,
So I'm speaking of mankind, and of what this team can do
If they both support each other and say, "I believe in you."

It's amazing how a person, though he thinks himself so
small,
When he knows someone's behind him can dig down and
give his all,
And sometimes surprise himself at what he now can do,
He has found this well of strength from an "I believe in
you."

Such a startling revelation, when you've done all you can
do,
To step back and see you've done all you really wanted to,
And you know you owe the thanks for these dreams of
yours come true
To the faith of all the people who said, "I believe in you."

Dr. Gregory Bell
1956 Olympic Gold Medallist
Long Jump

CHAPTER TWENTY

PROFOUND STATEMENT

As it has been said and so it is written
That which lies behind us
And that which lies before us
Is very tiny in comparison to
That which lies within us.

FINAL TIMEOUT

In all that you do, *live* a purposeful life.

Remember my Five Ls—
Live, Learn, Love, and Leave a Legacy

Hallie Bryant

Remember, It is neither my air
nor your air, it is our air.

The Magic of *That*

I am *that,*
You are *that,*
All of this is *that,*
And *that's* all there is.

[UNITY—HARMONY]

DeePak Chopra

GRAND FINALE

"To everything there is a season,
and a time to every purpose under heaven:"

ECCLESIASTES 3:1

It is written in the *Introduction* of this book that, "life is not one slam-dunk." We have illustrated this in many ways throughout the book, and here, at this particular point, is when it all comes together. There was a time to read, a time to think, a time to dream, and a time to act.

This is the time for us to act as we conclude this part of the journey—a time for the slam-dunk. Photograph N is a picture of Hallie with Fred "Curly" Neal strategizing over the final play of the game. With an amazing spontaneous burst of energy, "Curly" would climb on to the shoulders of Meadowlark Lemon. "Curly" would then finish-off the last play with the highly popularized slam-dunk, which was the appropriate time for the grand finale that signaled the end of each Globetrotter game and the end of this book.

"Curly" and "The Comet"

Photograph N

LIVING THE PRINCIPLES

Presented to Hallie by coach Don Odle in 1987.

"With Appreciation for 30 Years
Of Contribution To The
Basketball Camp"

Photograph O

GOD BLESS YOU, and GOD BLESS AMERICA

GLOSSARY OF HALLIEISMS

AT and T	Appropriate , Timely and Tasteful
BVAMS	Beliefs, Values, Assumptions, Memories
BOT	Build, Overcome, Tolerate
CBA	Conceive It, Believe It, Achieve It
DEW	Desire, Energy, Willingness
ERSCHB	Execution, Repetition, Successes, Confidence, Habit, Belief
False Self	The untamed lower self. The Little Me
FBI	Faith, Belief, Imagination
GAP	The pause, where silence is, and where we are receptive to the divine guidance.
Hallieisms	Acronyms, Acrostics, and Mnemonics to anchor principles, concepts, processes
Habits	Learned behavior—many times unconsciously
I Know	When Hallie was 3 years old, he named his dog I Know
IVVER	Idealize It, Verbalize It, Visualize It, Emotionalize It, and Realize It
LPL	Learn from the past, Plan for the future, Live in the now

MPWI	Make Peace With Imperfection
MUFIT	Mercy, Understanding, Forgiveness, Imagination, and Truth.
PBAFAR	Programming, Beliefs, Attitudes, Feelings, Action, Results
PEMSS	Physical, Emotional, Mental, Spiritual, Social PPUPP Peak Performance Under Peak Pressure (Bert Decker)
PUUR	Purposeful, Useful, Understandable, Relevant
R 2 A 2	Recognize, Relate, Assimilate, Apply
RBMG	Relax, Breathe, and Move Gracefully
SICO	Should've, If Only, Could've, Oh my God!
TFAR	Thoughts, Feelings, Action, Results
The 3 Cs	Complaining, Condemning, Criticizing
The 3 Fs and B	Focus, Flow, Flex, and Balance
The 4 Fs	Firm, Fair, Flexible, Frank
The 4 Rs	Review, Register, Recall, Retain
The 5 Ls	Live, Learn, Love, Leave a Legacy
The CODE	Coordination, Organization, Direction, Energy
True Self	The Real Self. In harmony with the Universe. The Big Me and Higher self
WOW	Well of Wisdom
YES!™	Your Energy Source™

ADDITIONAL RESOURCES

BOOKS

ALLEN JAMES. *As a Man Thinketh.* [NC]: De Vorss & Company, [ND].

ANTHONY, DR. ROBERT. *The Ultimate Secrets of Total Self-Confidence.* Beverly Hills: The Berkley Publishing Group, 1986.

BLOODWORTH, DR. J. VENICE. *The Key to Yourself.* Los Angeles: Schrivener and Company, 1975.

BUTCHEE, O'MERRIAL. *Phobophobia—The Fear of Fear.* Sevierville: Insigh Publishing, 1998.

CARLSON, RICHARD. *Don't Sweat the Small Stuff—It's All Small Stuff.* New York: Hyperion, 1997.

CARSON, RICHARD D. *Taming Your Gremlin.* New York: Harper Row Publishers, Inc., 1983.

CARTER, ARNOLD "NICK." *Communicate Effectively.* Gretna: Pelican Company, 1978.

COVEY, STEPHEN. *Living the Habits—7 Habits of Highly Effective People.* Provo: Covey Leadership Center, 1992.

DECKER, BERT. *You Have to Be Believed to Be Heard.* New York: St. Martin Press, 1992.

GANDHI, MAHATMA. *The Story of My Experiments with Truth.* Mineola: Dover Publications, Inc., 1983.

HELMSTETTER, SHADRICK. *What to Say When You Talk to Yourself.* New York: Simon & Schuster, Inc., 1982.

HILL, NAPOLEON. *Think and Grow Rich.* New York: Hawthorn Books, Inc., 1972.

HOWARD, VERNON. *Psycho-pictography.* West Nyack: Parker Publishing Company, 1965.

JOHNSON, DR. SPENCER and LARRY WILSON. *One Minute Salesperson.* New York: William Morrow Company, 1984.

KEYES, KEN, JR. *Handbook to Higher Consciousness.* Berkeley: The Living Love Center, 1972.

MALTZ, DR. MAXWELL. *Psycho-cybernetics.* Los Angeles: Prentice Hall, Inc., 1960.

MANDELLA, NELSON. *Long Walk to Freedom.* Boston: Little Brown & Co. 1995.

MANDINO, OG. *The Greatest Secret in the World.* New York: Frederick Fell Company, 1972.

STOOP, DR. DAVID. *Self-talk: Key to Personal Growth.* Old Tappan: Fleming H. Revel Company. 1982.

TAPES

The following tapes are from Nightingale-Conant, Chicago, IL:

AARON, BRUCE. *Gestalt Thinking Tape.*

CHOPRA, DR. DEEPAK. *Magical Mind, Magical Body.*

DYER, DR. WAYNE. *The Universe Within You.*

FINLEY, GUY. *The Power of the Free Mind.*

LARSEN, EARNIE. *The Transformed Self.*

NIGHTINGALE, EARL. *The Strangest Secret.*

ROHN, JIM. *Take Charge of Your Life.*

SIEGEL, DR. BERNIE. *Love, Medicine, and Miracles.*

TEMPLETON, CHARLES. *Succeeding.*

TICE, LOUIS. *Mastering the Attitude of Achievement.*

TRACY, BRIAN. *Thinking Big—The Key to Personal Power.*

WILLIAMSON, MARIANNE. *On Practical Spirituality.*

ABOUT THE AUTHOR

Hallie "The Comet" Bryant spent nearly three decades with the internationally-known Harlem Globetrotters organization, both as a player and in public relations. He delivers motivational and inspirational keynotes on success and conducts workshops and seminars that will help anyone who desires to have a winning edge in life.

Through audience participation, Hallie creates a fun atmosphere on how to develop a harmonious lifestyle based on his Win-Win Theory, Self-talk, and Self-management. He has appeared before Eli Lilly, U.S.

Department of Customs, General Motors, General Electric, The Special Olympics, Sherwin-Williams, and at hundreds of other community groups and large corporations and institutions of higher learning.

Hallie is a graduate of Indiana University and since serving as a commissioned officer in the U.S. Army has become a Certified Self-Talk Trainer from the Helmstetter Self-Talk Institute and has appeared on several national television shows, performed during NBA halftimes and served as a special sports commentator for CBS. In addition to Hallie's extremely busy schedule as a keynote speaker, he is the Honorary Chairperson for the Memory Walk 2002 for the Alzheimer's Association and the spokesperson for the Dyslexia Institute of Indiana, Inc.

ABOUT THE CO-AUTHOR

O'Merrial Butchee is an international speaker, author and successful business leader. She is the president and CEO of Visionamics, Inc, a national consulting and training firm. Her company specializes in diversity and leadership training. In her highly interactive, fast-paced seminars and keynotes, Ms. Butchee shares more than twenty years of her practical experiences in diversity, business and leadership development.

As a past treasurer of a Fortune 100 company, she managed a division portfolio in excess of $80 million.

Because she is the "big picture thinker" she stimulates her audiences to operate outside of the box. Her clients and participants are from Fortune 500 companies and national organizations, and associations such as Coldwell Banker, Indiana University, Kraft Foods, Northwestern Mutual Life Insurance Company, and the Environmental Protection Agency.

She has a master's degree in Public and Environmental Affairs, and has received various degrees and certifications from institutions such as Purdue University, La Universidad Ibero-Americana—Mexico, and the National Association of Credit Management. She was nominated the Speaker of the Year 2000 by the National African American Speakers Association. Some of her other affiliations are the International Platform Association and the National Speakers Association.

158.1 B 84

Hallie's comet :